OTHER TITLES IN SERIES

**The High School Principal and Staff
Work Together**

by Elwood L. Prestwood

**The High School Principal and Staff
Study Youth**

by Glyn Morris

**The High School Principal and Staff
Deal with Discipline**

by Ovid Parody

**SECONDARY SCHOOL ADMINISTRATION SERIES**

**David B. Austin, Editor**

# THE HIGH SCHOOL PRINCIPAL AND STAFF

# Plan for Program Improvement

**PAUL M. MITCHUM**
Assistant Superintendent of Schools
Wilmington, Delaware

BUREAU OF PUBLICATIONS  1958

Teachers College, Columbia University, New York

PRINTED IN THE UNITED STATES OF AMERICA

# *Editor's Introduction*

EDUCATION of American youth is a national concern largely controlled at the local level of decision-making and legally the responsibility of the various states. This apparent confusion is actually a source of strength because it allows for refinement of the program of instruction to be made by those most closely associated with the ones to be taught in the actual setting in which the learning is accomplished.

Such circumstances place an unusual responsibility directly in the hands of the staff of local school systems and individual schools. It has therefore become an integral part of the work of teachers and administrators, as they perform their professional functions, to deal with the critical matter of constantly developing—and improving—the program of instruction. This is best accomplished through careful cooperative effort.

In the following pages Dr. Mitchum describes a procedure which has proved successful. It was derived from daily practice in the field and from the findings of recent as well as long-established researches. The result will be of direct help to faculties and administrators who face the constant challenges of making meaningful the program of learning for modern American youth.

Dr. Mitchum writes against a background of success as a classroom teacher, a school principal, and a central office administrator whose major responsibility is the developing program of instruction of a school system. His experience has been distinguished by his remarkable ability to draw upon the best products of planned research and apply them to the daily problems of the teaching profession. Thus, here is a monograph of substance, designed to help devoted teachers and administrators improve their skills in accomplishing the fundamental task of the profession through continuous co-operative study of the program of youth education which they develop.

Lest there be any misunderstanding, let it be clearly stated that no actual program is herewith offered. Rather, contributing to the unique strength of the schools of our country, this book will facilitate the evolution of a better and better curriculum as determined best by those responsible for senior and junior high schools.

DAVID B. AUSTIN
Professor of Education
Teachers College, Columbia University

# Contents

# Chapter 1

## WHAT KIND OF PRINCIPAL LEADERSHIP IS MOST
## CONDUCIVE TO PROGRAM IMPROVEMENT?

PRINCIPAL–TEACHER relationships are discussed at length in other monographs of this series, but it is pertinent here to review some of the more critical characteristics of these relationships as they impinge upon the problem of this particular monograph. Any plan for program improvement will succeed or fail according to how well the principal and staff work together.

1. The principal should be sure that he and his teachers know and understand each other. The very fact that curriculum change, to be effective, must inevitably take place in the classroom requires mutual respect and consideration between staff and leader. Each should have confidence in the other's good intentions; they should speak the same language or at least each should understand the language the other speaks.

"Now I want this matter to have thorough discussion" may be the principal's invitation for the staff's careful consideration of an issue, or it may simply be a cue for all those who agree with the principal to make their agreement known. Likewise, when faculty members indicate approval of a proposal they may in effect be pledging their energies and skills to the successful completion of the proposal; on the other hand, they may simply be showing their willingness for the principal to try carrying it out.

Furthermore, a spirit of willingness and co-operation may exist between leader and staff members without an identity of understanding of the precise meaning of a particular proposition or issue. Such terms as pupil responsibility, student government, promptness, pre-planning, objectives, activity period, voluntary choice, parents' approval, evaluation, conference, agreement, and study period may not only mean many things to many different people but they may also mean different things to the same people at different times. Much staff time can be consumed with problems which no longer exist after the meaning of terms is made clear.

Similarly, faculty agreement can be fruitless if it develops that different members were agreeing to different interpretations of an issue. Actually, words can be devised and arranged which elicit agreement but conceal basic conflicts. The statement "We believe boys and girls should be given opportunities to develop individual responsibility" may be interpreted by one teacher as suggesting situations in which the pupil is encouraged to make his own decisions. Another teacher may feel that this statement means providing ample opportunity for the pupil to follow directions faithfully.

Unfortunately, too, words can be arranged which seem to say one thing but actually mean the opposite. "I agree one hundred per cent with what has been said but I would just like to add . . . , "or "I like Miss Smith's suggestion but I would like to ask just one question . . . ," or "That's a wonderful idea but from an administrative standpoint . . ." may simply be a polite prelude to an emphatic disagreement.

A faculty's progress depends considerably upon the members' ability to communicate clearly and adequately with one another. To do his part in achieving staff understanding, the principal will have to establish more than a casual acquaintance with faculty members. He should know them as individuals; he should find out a great deal about their training, background, and personality characteristics. Thus, through his knowledge of the members of the staff with which he works, and through their deeper acquaintance with him, the critical problems of mutual understanding and confidence can be resolved.

2. The principal should be solicitous about and respectful of staff members' viewpoints. He should show that he is not solely

concerned with advancing his own views and objectives. A faculty cannot really be sure of this point until they have discovered that their leader has refrained from pursuing a personally prized objective because he recognizes that the staff as a whole cannot accept that objective as their own. For example, a principal may feel that the school's marking system should be less competitive than it is. If the staff are aware of this but realize that the principal will not force his preferences against dominant staff opinion, then they will have greater confidence in group thinking and planning.

The teachers in a given school may have had a sad experience with a principal who has demonstrated his inability to modify his personal position in relation to school issues. Such teachers, no matter how much talk there is to the contrary, cannot be expected to produce good teamwork or to bring about significant changes in the curriculum. Although the principal who insists on thinking *for* the staff instead of thinking *with* the staff can secure a certain degree of compliance with the changes made and even acceptance of them, he is assuming a considerable burden of proof of the all-knowing, all-wise leader, and he is denying the teachers an opportunity to think for themselves.

The principal can show his concern for individual teachers' views and opinions by encouraging each one to state his views in meetings and by insisting that the whole staff weigh all proposals and expressions carefully. It is especially important that encouragement be given to the teacher whose view is markedly different from the trend of discussion or who may have information not yet presented. Also, in personal conversations the principal's response to a teacher's expression of opinion which does not agree with his own may reveal the extent of his willingness to consider opposing views. If the principal as leader wants his own ideas weighed carefully, then he must see to it that all staff members' ideas are considered fairly and carefully.

3. The principal should help teachers reach beyond their present stage of thinking and professional development. As he presents ideas and suggestions, or as he reacts to suggestions of staff members, it should be clear that his ideas stand or fall on

their inherent good sense and persuasiveness and not on the authority of his position. Nonetheless, he should not evade his responsibility to stimulate and challenge faculty thinking. He should insist on the application of reasoned judgment, adequate data, and philosophical consistency to the consideration of school problems. He is not a true leader if he is content to be a counter of noses, a peacemaker, or an opponent of change.

Obviously, the principal's approach to leadership should be supported by his own careful study and reflection. He cannot lead others toward professional growth unless he has engaged in frequent personal reappraisal of his own outlook and his own techniques. Does the principal permit his habits of schedule making, teacher assignment, or general office routine to prevent consideration of change? How often is he heard to say, "It won't work administratively"? Are faculty meetings routine and unplanned, or do they really grapple with educational issues and problems? Program improvement implies program change. The program cannot be changed unless the people working with it change. The principal himself must learn to grow professionally and to change if he expects to succeed in getting teachers to grow professionally.

4. The principal must accept his responsibility for program improvement. The Committee on the Role of the Principal of the Philadelphia Suburban School Study Council has stated its conviction that improvement of instruction is the principal's most important responsibility.[1] In line with its conviction, this committee has recommended that principals in its member schools abandon the open-door policy in favor of a planned and structured work day, one in which definite clock time is set aside for the principal to be out in the classrooms.

This same committee, after much thought and discussion, was not willing to see the principal delegate his leadership in program improvement. He might share his leadership and he might dele-

[1] Philadelphia Suburban School Study Council, Group A, *The Leadership Role of the Principal*, p. 3. Philadelphia: Educational Service Bureau, School of Education, University of Pennsylvania, 1956.

gate many of the tasks, but he should not delegate his responsibility. Perhaps the most potent argument for the principal's assuming generalship of curriculum improvement is that he thus demonstrates to the faculty his conviction that this task has top priority. If one agrees with the Suburban Philadelphia group that the most important responsibility of the principal is improvement of instruction (what do *you* think is the principal's greatest responsibility?), then it follows that the principal must structure not only his work *day* but also his work *year* for leadership of staff activities which are designed to build a better school program.

How many secretaries and vice-principals must a school have in order for the principal to be free to assume his role of leadership in curriculum improvement? The answer is that there are not enough secretaries and vice-principals in the whole world to get a principal to do what he has not accepted as a chief responsibility in the first place. No matter how many things are stacked on a principal's desk, program improvement can be either at the bottom of the stack or at the top of the stack. The writer realizes that many secondary schools are understaffed and that many principals are badgered by seemingly endless demands upon their time. The difficulty of a principal's engineering his work time so that he can take active leadership of curriculum development in his school does not diminish its importance. Acceptance of the responsibility is the first step toward meeting the responsibility.

5. Leadership should be shared. The principal, once he has accepted responsibility for it, does not have to carry the entire burden. If he has shown by action and attitude that he works co-operatively with the staff, that he is more interested in group thinking than in the advocacy of personal views, then there should be an opportunity for faculty members to develop *their* resourcefulness and to increase their skills as responsible group members. The kind of leadership most conducive to program improvement is shared leadership. This involves intelligent and responsible participation by faculty members and is dependent on the principal's willingness to have a shared leadership. Each individual's right to exert influence should be recognized. Group thinking should

be the medium through which goals are set up and group action the means of achieving them.

Shared leadership must go from teacher to principal and from teacher to teacher as well as from principal to teacher. If someone on the staff has demonstrated, or wants to demonstrate, his leadership skills in attacking a particular school problem, the principal should be willing to sit as a group member. To those status leaders who are afraid they will lose something by stepping down from the presiding chair—though the writer has never been able to decide what is thus lost—it should be said that what is gained is infinitely greater. The good leader is also a good follower. He knows that if staff leadership is to develop, individuals must have an opportunity to grow.

Even when leadership does emerge from within a faculty, an otherwise good principal may be tempted to share everything but the credit for what the faculty achieves. It is so traditional for reports and accounts of school life to issue from the principal's office that sometimes community members get the impression that the principal personally does all those wonderful things. Good principals make it a practice to mention teachers' names in publicity dealing with school life. Some have followed the practice of writing thank-you notes to individual teachers who have performed certain tasks. Others are careful in staff meetings to give credit to those teachers who are responsible for certain achievements.

The writer recalls how surprised he was several years ago at the effect of a personal expression of thanks to a teacher. As he was standing at the school bus loading station, the writer sincerely, but casually, mentioned his appreciation of the good work being done by the teacher who was supervising the bus loading. The next morning this teacher came especially to the office to say, "You know, I've been supervising the bus loading for ten years and yesterday afternoon was the first time *anybody* has bothered to thank me for it!" It may be that principals need to give more attention to sharing the credit than to any other aspect of shared leadership.

6. The principal should be a member of the professional leadership team of his school system. He has an obligation to understand and work with the superintendent and other system-wide personnel. Much will be said in this monograph about the principal's relationship to other leaders. The principal should help develop system-wide policies and should help secure their observance by the faculty of his school. He should welcome participation by system-wide leaders in his school's activities.

7. The principal should be willing to work with parents in gaining their understanding and support of the school's program. Parents can hardly be expected to support that which they have not even heard explained. This point is discussed in Chapter 6.

8. A definite commitment to the democratic concept of administration should accompany a principal's desire to accomplish what has been set forth in this chapter. Has he made a clear-cut choice between democratic administration and autocratic administration? If a principal or other school leader is inclined to be an autocrat, he has the machinery at his disposal to be just that. There are school systems in which this form of leadership prevails. Outwardly, the organization may seem the same as that in other school systems; inwardly, the general outlook and ways of working can be quite different. Action rather than pronouncement is the test of administrative belief.

Actually, there are at least two other kinds of school administration which one may encounter. One is the benevolent-despot type, in which the leader may be generous, inspiring, and considerate without sharing the privileges and responsibilities of leadership with his staff. He may even traffic with a degree of democratic machinery, proclaim a faith in democracy, but nonetheless direct and control everything personally. Some of these leaders apparently fool themselves into thinking they are truly democratic. One should perhaps hesitate to suggest that others in this group of leaders frankly pervert democratic machinery and processes. Whether their understandings or their motives are at fault, the results in either case are not desirable if public schools have an obligation to prepare boys and girls for intelligent participation in a democratic society. The identifying characteristic of many such administrators is the consistency with which decisions apparently made by the faculty coincide with the principal's personal convictions and wishes.

A fourth kind of school leadership is the laissez-faire. Here may be a leader who has never settled down to developing an intelligent concept of leadership. Perhaps he solves problems on a day-to-day basis without bothering to consider whether the solutions add up to a consistent philosophy. He is not inclined to disturb matters that don't disturb him. If a problem is not screaming for attention, perhaps it doesn't exist. If an issue can be postponed, perhaps it will go away. The laissez-faire leader, however, may have considerable devotion to democratic values but just can't bring himself to pay the price required to put them into practice. If he happens to be surrounded by staff members who can put democratic values into practice, much progress may follow. Too often, though, the laissez-faire principal is surrounded by other laissez-faire people or, worse yet, by schemers and plotters who thrive in such an environment. There is not likely to be teamwork or effective group action in this working situation or under the despot, be he benevolent or otherwise.

Democratic administration provides the most encouraging environment for the principal and the staff to work together for program improvement. The role of leadership should be thought through carefully; it should be consistent in outlook and practice.

It has been suggested in this chapter, then, that leadership which produces effective curriculum change meets the following requirements:

1. The principal and the staff understand each other.
2. The principal respects staff members' viewpoints.
3. The principal stimulates teachers' professional growth.
4. The principal accepts responsibility for program improvement.
5. The principal shares leadership.
6. The principal works as a member of a leadership team.

7. The principal secures co-operation of parents in program change.

8. The principal is committed to the democratic concept of administration.

Democratic leadership, shared leadership, emerging leadership should pervade all phases of school life. If the most significant curriculum changes are to take place—changes significant in schools of a democratic society—they must occur in the day-to-day living, planning, and achieving of school people as well as through organized, co-operative attacks on long-term issues.

Chapter *2*

## WHAT CONDITIONS SHOULD PREVAIL WHEN THE PRINCIPAL AND STAFF WORK ON PROGRAM IMPROVEMENT?

IT was suggested in Chapter 1 that a wholesome working relationship between the principal and staff is a prerequisite to effective group planning and group action. In other words, the principal's leadership should be established. It should not be status leadership which is inherent in his position, but *earned* leadership which comes only from recognition by the staff that the principal seeks and considers staff members' ideas, that leadership is shared, that credit is given where credit is due, and that the principal and other staff members are working toward common objectives by agreed-upon methods.

### Faculty Committees

In a school with such leadership, definite organization exists to provide for and encourage teacher responsibility. Preferably, teachers help set up the committee system of the school. In one school in which the writer worked, the teachers reorganized sixteen standing staff committees (previously established and appointed by the principal) into five new committees which met more often and more regularly because of almost no overlapping in personnel. In a large school, much of the routine work of a faculty can be expedited by an advisory committee of representative teachers. Although the principal may be tempted to appoint people whom he judges to be quite competent, teacher sense of participation is more likely to be enhanced if at least part of the committee is selected by the teachers themselves. Representatives may be chosen at large, by grade levels, by departments, or even by sections of the building. The size of such a committee will vary with the size of the school and the tasks to be accomplished. It is helpful at the outset to limit the duration of an advisory committee member's tenure, so that over a period of years a considerable number of teachers will have experience on the committee. The faculty may also want to set up additional rules to insure a fair distribution of sex, age groups, and subject areas.

Staff meetings are not devoted exclusively to administrative announcements nor do they consume an excessive amount of time with the "democratic" consideration of insignificant items. Teachers are accustomed to staff meetings built around professional problems, developed and presented by teacher groups. The principal does not depend upon staff-at-large meetings alone for the professional growth of teachers. He frequently meets with small groups of teachers interested in identical or similar problems. In both small and large groups of teachers there is a maximum of co-operative effort and a minimum of power struggles and personality flare-ups. Conclusions are not reached before pertinent facts are gathered. Minority rights are respected, but the minority does not expect veto power over dominant staff opinion. There is little formal voting, especially on issues, because the desire is to talk through, think through, and work through the issues of a problem until the staff-at-large is satisfied that the best possible solution under the circumstances has been reached. In such a working environment, surely a principal's leadership is established, recognized, and respected.

## The Newcomer

A principal, of course, cannot expect his earned leadership to be established in the first days of his tenure; a period of time is required for getting acquainted with people as well as problems.

If a new principal is fortunate enough to inherit a situation in which a staff is already moving forward, in which members are working together, in which staff studies are well organized and in progress, he will surely want to encourage the continuance of such a happy situation. This means again, however, that he will want to take several months just to get acquainted before he plunges into the midst of things; otherwise he may be more in the way than helpful. Meanwhile, it is hoped that the school staff will continue the momentum initiated through previous leadership.

If the new principal inherits a situation in which a staff is not moving forward, even more time will be required for the establishment of his earned leadership. If the staff is unaware that it is not moving along, then the most time of all will be required. Complacency can be deep-rooted, especially if a faculty has been unaccustomed to professional study or to being invited to share in the planning and thinking. Under such circumstances, the new principal will do well initially to seek ways and means of improving working relationships among faculty members through work on operational problems rather than through comprehensive curriculum study.

In those exciting cases in which a new principal and new staff start out together, such as in the opening of a new school, it is to be hoped that there has been a period of time for preparatory and planning work by staff and principal. The necessity of getting the new school into operation, the thrill of a new environment, the anticipation of new experiences will tend to give unity to a faculty which will carry over as members get better acquainted with their jobs and with one another. When the pupil population and the staff of a new school are housed in an older school until the new plant is ready, the principal of the new school may be assigned as an administrative assistant in the existing school. This will give him an opportunity to establish some of his leadership while his school is still in the planning stage. When a new principal and staff start out together, leadership can be shared as it is developed. Staff responsibility grows along with recognition of the principal's leadership.

We have been saying, then, that the principal and staff should not consider extensive curriculum change until the principal's leadership is established and there is a firm, wholesome working relationship among the staff.

## Points of Departure

Another prerequisite to projects of curriculum change is for the principal and staff to feel that there are some inadequacies in the existing program. It is difficult to lead a faculty toward or into curriculum change if there prevails a smug satisfaction with things as they are. Almost any school, however good it may be, will have problems which are quite obvious to teachers; but these problems may not necessarily be classified as curriculum problems, at least in their initial aspects. If there are excessive dropouts, if certain subject offerings are losing their popularity, if teachers find existing courses of study too restrictive, if some pupils find courses too difficult and others find them not challenging, if counselors feel that some of the behavior problems stem from classroom learning situations, then the staff will look with favor on ways and means of seeking improvement.

Furthermore, there is hardly any school-life problem or group of problems which, if pursued vigorously enough, will not have some bearing on curriculum. Discipline problems, for instance, may in their early phases demand the establishment of "law and order" in a given classroom or other school situation. Once classroom order is established, however, the continuance of it will depend in a large measure on the effectiveness of the learning situation in that classroom. This in turn will depend on the readiness of the learner for what is to be learned.

One high school staff became quite upset over the pupils' evident lack of good judgment in school elections. At first this problem appeared to the teachers to be one of citizenship, one of behavior. Then they suddenly realized that virtually no opportunity was being provided by the school for learning good judgment which could be employed in school elections. Closer study also revealed that many homeroom elections were no better in quality than school-wide elections. Improvement was brought about when social studies teachers took time out from studying the Battle of Wilson Creek (Missouri) and discussed with their pupils the qualifications of school leaders and how to exercise good choices in school elections. Classroom experiences were set up in which pupils put into practice the principles they had studied. Thereafter in that school social studies teachers each year included a unit of study on the intelligent choice of school leaders. Thus, school life problems tend to blend into curriculum problems.

## System-Wide Relationships

A desirable aid in the pursuit of curriculum study is the support and encouragement of the central office. While financial resources of the central office are very helpful, it is even more important that central office personnel have at least an advisory relationship with a study being pursued in a given school. Above all, the principal should be sure that the superintendent approves the study proposal and its predictable outcomes, especially if other school units are affected or if critical issues are likely to be raised in the minds of community members. In addition, in a large school system there will be other personnel, such as directors of instruction and supervisors, who can be of considerable assistance but whose lack of co-operation might bright frustration.

The following comments are part of a stenographic record of a meeting of a junior high school staff committee with the superintendent of schools, the curriculum director, the director of secondary education, and two parents. The staff committee was explaining the junior high school's seventh grade program to system-wide leaders.

*Curriculum Director:* Is there flexibility in your general education program?

*Vice-principal:* Yes, flexibility in that one group may remain more than 12 weeks in crafts, foods, or shop if that group is working on a project and needs more time to finish it.

*Superintendent:* What is the basis for grouping children?

*Teacher A:* Groups are set up on the basis of their ability for living with one another.

*Principal:* Teachers group children on the basis of what they consider to be a workable group.

*Superintendent:* I have known some people who can live together but they don't accomplish much.

*Principal:* We put some pupils together in the same group so they will learn to adjust themselves to society.

*Teacher B:* Some of the factors we take into account in grouping pupils are: (1) Band and orchestra pupils have to be in the same group. (2) We try to have an equal number of boys and girls. (3) We try to have a representative range of ability in each group. (4) We try to keep apart students who would consistently cause trouble for the group.

*Curriculum Director:* How do you face the problem of a child who does not get along with the group?

*Principal:* According to the traditional school of thought the child had to conform to the group. Now we take the child's outlook into consideration as well as the teacher's viewpoint and the group's welfare. Sometimes a child can get along with one group when he can't adjust to another.

*Teacher C:* Shifting the child from one group to another is the last thing that is done, not the first.

*Principal:* We group children from previous experience too. Before the children come over from the sixth grade we talk with their elementary principals before grouping them in the seventh grade.

*Vice-principal:* When a child enters our school from another school or from out of town, the dean of boys and I always have a conference with him before placing him with any certain group.

*Dean of Boys:* When we group a pupil we take into consideration his ideas.

*Director of Secondary Education:* Can you change a student from one group to another according to your schedule?

*Vice-principal:* Yes.

*Principal:* We think we ought to have more parent participation in all this planning.

*Curriculum Director:* You should set up certain limitations for the areas of discussion with parents; otherwise meetings may not be constructive.

*Superintendent:* You are putting more emphasis on living together rather than on learning the basic skills. Parents that I know always want to know what the child can do. Can he add and subtract and so on? A child needs this basic knowledge in order to obtain a job.

*Vice-principal:* According to a student committee which reflects the ideas of parents, they are more interested in citizenship.

*Principal:* Mrs. ———, what is your opinion?

*Parent:* Parents are inclined not to interfere with the school's program unless their child is having some difficulty.

*Principal:* We are not ignoring the basic skills but are trying to bring them into the program in a more meaningful way. The program varies according to grade levels.

The reader will note that in this brief portion of a staff's conference with central office leaders certain concerns of the different personnel are revealed. It will also be noted that the parent assumed a wait-and-see attitude. It was apparent that the staff did the right thing in arranging this conference with central leaders. Later in this meeting the staff committee asked the central office leaders if the school's program was consistent with system-wide policies and objectives. Central leaders suggested some modifications of the school's plans and these changes were adopted. Both the staff and the central office personnel were identified with the amended program.

If the current experience in a given school system shows that there is good rapport between central office personnel on the one hand and school unit administrators on the other, the question of central office support is not difficult. However, if the school units have not been accustomed to carrying on curriculum studies and central personnel have been busy in their offices, it seems obvious that careful exploratory planning with central personnel is incumbent upon a principal whose staff is considering venturing into an extensive project of program improvement.

## Courageous Inquiry and Consequences

Another important exploratory activity before a staff moves far into a curriculum study is that of agreeing upon purposes and establishing goals. At first thought one might assume that these could be developed as the study progresses, but some matters should be considered in advance. One critical factor is the question of whether the staff and the school system are prepared to accept and act on possible findings of the proposed study. For instance, if the teachers in a school have been accustomed to following prescribed courses of study scrupulously and some teachers should ask to be freed from course of study requirements in order to move the study along faster, what answer are they going to be given? Again, if a member of one of the subject departments reports that he would like to try out a certain experiment in connection with the study, but his department chairman is opposed to it, what answer will be given? Still again, suppose a group of teachers proposes to arrange all the tenth grade classrooms in one wing of the building instead of having the classrooms arranged strictly by subject areas, will such a recommendation be given careful study? What would happen to a recommendation that classroom libraries be set up and that the school central library be decentralized? What if teachers decide that the class period should be lengthened or the activity period abolished or that all pupils at all grade levels should be required to take fine arts? These are just samples of questions which can arise as a faculty begins to break away from established patterns. On a different subject, but dealing with planning, more than one superintendent has been dismayed with a faculty's frustration over the necessity of modifying dream plans for a new building to fit financial realities. Similar frustration can occur in curriculum planning if there has not been a careful look ahead at probable costs, changes, and outcomes.

This all points to the advisability of a staff's having at least a general notion of a destination for a study of program improvement. There should be some generally agreed upon concept of the secondary school's role in a democratic society lest the study become aimless and unproductive. It is not suggested that a curriculum study always be preceded by a full-dress study of school philosophy—many school shelves are groaning under the weight of countless copies of neatly duplicated statements of philosophy. There are times when a school faculty needs to move or make a change even though there is no absolute certainty of the outcome. Just to find that one can break away from long-established habits and patterns can be exhilarating. Nonetheless, a school cannot go on indefinitely studying change without relating the change to certain understood and agreed upon goals. These goals must relate to what a school staff accepts as the school's role in the school community and to what the staff (and pupils and community) believe the school's obligation to the pupil to be.

If it has not been spelled out in so many words thus far, it should be clearly stated now that a staff and principal should not consider entering any extensive curriculum study unless the study will be given the necessary priority to prevent it from being forgotten or neglected. Nothing will kill a study more completely than to have it postponed, overlooked, or superseded by other matters. Once begun, it should be followed through to completion or to some definite point, or it should not be started at all. Teacher time and effort should not be dissipated on projects which dwindle into nothingness. While this is true of all staff projects, curriculum or otherwise, it is particularly critical for curriculum studies because they deal with the basic center of a school's existence, namely, what goes on in the classrooms.

Before the principal and staff proceed very far into a study of program improvement, then, it is suggested that these questions be considered:

1. Is the principal's earned leadership established and do principal and staff work well together?
2. In the case of a new principal, do the problems of his orientation and the nature of the staff situation which he inherits warrant his attempting to lead his new staff into curriculum study at this time?
3. Is the staff aware of inadequacies in the present program?
4. Will the central office support the study and its predictable outcomes?
5. Does the school staff have some understanding of goals and curriculum objectives, a sense of direction?
6. Can the program be given enough priority that it will be followed through and not neglected?

It is not necessary that the answers to all these questions be at the same starting line at the same time. If, however, there is not at least one of these questions to which the principal and staff can give a positive answer, then curriculum study of any significant nature should not be pursued in that school at this time.

Lack of positive answer to some of these questions should not deter a principal from working toward a staff relationship which *will* permit curriculum study. The establishment of new ways of working, the stimulation of critical thinking, the encouragement of an experimental attitude, the removal of conditions which have blocked faculty progress should challenge the principal and the staff to courageous action.

# Chapter 3

## HOW SHOULD THE PROBLEM BE FORMULATED?

THERE will be times in a faculty's experience when no effort has to be exerted to discover a problem justifying intensive study. One will emerge clearly from school life activities or from sudden or marked changes in normal, accustomed patterns. A rapid change in the characteristics of school enrollment can make it imperative for a school to modify its program. Occupying a new building will almost surely cause a faculty to look seriously at its curriculum offerings, especially if the faculty has shared in planning the building.

Sometimes too, a ready-made problem has been furnished by a previous staff study or a previous year's work. A study of the seventh grade clubs one year might naturally suggest a study of clubs for other grades the following year. A study of school marks may have uncovered the need for better parent contacts. A study of community resources may have pointed up the need for helping community members better understand the school's program. A study of vocational education may have suggested needed improvements in the English offerings for vocational students.

There will be other times when no problem is paramount or evident or when there are so many problems that a choice has to be made. Since people are not always aggressive about problems which nonetheless may be critical to them, it might be advisable at intervals to take a faculty census of the problems which appear important to the members. One junior high school principal mailed out to all staff members shortly before the September opening of school a request for a listing of such problems. Teachers were asked to suggest *school* problems and then check the ones which were problems to them *personally*. Responses fell into the categories of discipline, pupil achievement, parent relationships, and curriculum structure. It should be added that this particular school had a well-advanced curriculum program and the teachers were not only accustomed to working on curriculum problems but usually had one or more curriculum projects lined up for the future.

A problem census, of course, may be taken once or several times during a school year. A check list often is used or teachers may be asked to write down what occurs to them. Some faculties have started a problem census with free responses of teachers the first round and a check list based on the first responses for the second round.

The following unedited list of school problems was collected from ten teacher discussion groups at Upper Darby, Pennsylvania, Junior High School. A total of eighty-nine staff members participated in these discussion groups; each group held two sessions in which problems were suggested.

* How can our staff deal with the problem of the reputation of being rebels which we seem to have in some quarters?
* How can we improve discipline in the corridors? Can the standard set by the "minute men" be improved?

Is it possible and desirable to keep children from entering the building before class time in the morning?

Is an advisory committee necessary for our staff? Might it not tend to short-circuit thinking of the staff as a whole?

° Is democratic administration dangerous? Is democratic administration really democratic; that is, can it work without someone taking unfair advantage? Might the principal later find himself in conflict with staff opinion in matters which are of critical importance?

* What is the role of the minority on a staff like ours? What are its privileges and obligations? Same questions for the majority.
* How can we arrive at decisions by consensus instead of by voting?
* What are some of the obligations of membership in a group; that is, who should be the compromiser, the expediter, the catalyst, the summarizer, the advocate, the peacemaker?
* Is there a fair distribution of assignments to cover classes of teachers who are absent?
* How can we improve communication in our school? Notices to

teachers have not been received in all cases; should we post notices in the rest rooms?

*What about gym night? Can it be whittled down a bit? Will there ever be a time when we don't have it?

What about homework? Is there some way to distribute it so that a pupil does not have too much of it at one time? How can we explain homework to parents?

Is there some way to keep loafers out of the balcony after school? To what extent have pupils been loitering there?

*What about air-raid drills? Are we prepared?

Could we get students from senior high school to operate the duplicator for teachers during the last period?

*Should we have student receptionists at our front doorway during the school day?

What about our club program?

*Can we devise a better way of arranging our lunch periods? Is it necessary to have pupils sit in the auditorium?

What are the real educational purposes of assemblies?

Should we continue to have tag day?

Is there some way to plan a schedule so that coaches could have free periods on Friday afternoons when the games take place?

*What is the future of our junior high school? What kind of school would we have if we had only grades seven and eight? How can we relieve crowded conditions here if we keep some of the ninth grade next year?

What about the direction of traffic flow in corridors between classes? Is there any way we can improve on the present plan?

What about traffic tie-up in front of our building on bad weather days? Can we find more space for parents' cars when parents come to pick up children?

*Can we do a better job of teaching reading? How can we convince pupils of the necessity of learning to read well?

Are we making the best use of our television set?

Does girls' physical education get the consideration it should have?

What should we try to accomplish in homeroom? What is the homeroom for?

It will be noted that there is considerable range of complexity and significance among the different items in the above list. During the one and a half school years following the compilation of the list, the items starred received consideration and some action was taken. Pursuit of the item on reading resulted in a post-school study group the following June, in which twenty-five staff members participated. All of these projects were approved by the faculty at large. Even though a faculty committee may recommend the final choice of problems to be studied, it is important that the staff at large make the final decision, thus identifying it as a faculty-wide study and not just the concern of a committee.

## Sources of Problems

Standing committees of a faculty may also evolve or state problems which a faculty will want to pursue. A guidance committee may want the faculty to look at elective and required courses. An activities committee may propose that physical education classes take over responsibility for developing activities which were formerly of an extra-class nature. A standing committee on curriculum may suggest experimentation in certain areas.

Another source of curriculum study suggestions is system-wide leadership. Central leadership in the Wilmington, Delaware, public schools initiated a three-year study of the superior student and asked all school units to participate after the first year of exploratory study by a system-wide committee. Principals were assigned the responsibility of developing the project in their own schools, but they were given assistance from the central office personnel.

If system-wide leadership has provided workshops, institutes, and other such professional growth activities for teachers, problems may develop in these activities which member school staffs may want to pursue. For example, if a summer workshop has been organized around child development, teachers who attend that workshop may exert influence the following school year for their own staff to modify its program in terms of new concepts.

Again, pressures from the community may cause a high school to look at various phases of its program. Rapid expansion of industry may accentuate the need for a diversified occupations program. Church groups may clamor for more attention to moral and spiritual values. Safety groups may advocate driver-training. Physical fitness organizations may want physical education taught every day instead of two periods per week. A local bank may want savings taught through a pupil savings bank plan. To answer such demands may require staff study.

Regional study groups offer member school staffs the opportunity of comparing notes with staffs of similar schools. Information is exchanged and frequently help is obtained from consultant staffs of universities. Mention has already been made of the Philadelphia suburban study on the role of the principal, in which ten school systems participated. The Philadelphia Suburban School Study Council is but one of several such groups in the nation. The 1954 manual of the National Conference of School Study Councils[1] lists thirty-three study councils in the United States for the school year 1954–55. These councils are located in all parts of the country. The manual defines a study council as

> . . . an organization of public school systems which have banded together to meet their problems in a more efficient manner. While there are some problems which must be faced on the local level, there are probably more problems, in both number and significance, which are faced better on a regional basis. A study council invariably has its central office in a college or university and has an executive officer who is a member of the college or university staff. The council is usually governed by a board of elected school people, usually administrators. Member schools pay varying amounts of dues for membership and for the different services which are provided. In a sentence, then, a study council is a voluntary organization of public schools, sponsored by an educational institution, governed by public school people with professional leadership in an effort to solve the recurring problems of education.[2]

Such study councils are especially helpful if the problems they tackle have come from the staffs of the affiliated schools. Several councils produce publications, some of them on a regular basis, which can be obtained from the sponsoring college or university director.

Regional study groups are not all confined to suburban or city school systems nor do they necessarily have to be affiliated with

---

[1] Daniel E. Griffiths, Editor, *How School Study Councils Work.* Albany, New York State College for Teachers, 1954.

[2] *Ibid.*, Foreword.

a college or university, though that is certainly desirable when possible. County organizations, as well as other geographical groupings, can enable school staffs to pool their resources with other school systems. Secondary school principals in a number of southwest Missouri counties follow the practice of having dinner together once a month, after which there is discussion of mutual problems. Items for consideration are agreed upon in advance and some principals bring other staff members to the meetings when the matters under study relate to interests or competencies of those particular teachers.

One of the interesting developments in this Missouri discussion group was the number of cases in which a principal whose own staff had dismissed a proposed practice as impossible and not worthy of trial would hear some other principal relate long and successful experience in the same practice.[3]

Several of the affiliated state groups of the National Association of Secondary-School Principals have sponsored discussion groups on a regional basis. There should be nothing to prevent principals and other teachers from setting up informal discussion on problems which are concerns of staff members from neighboring schools in near-by towns. Faculties can take turns playing host or perhaps a college in the vicinity will offer its facilities for a meeting place.

## The Principal's Role

The question may be asked: Is it not appropriate for the principal himself to suggest study problems for the faculty? In his position of leadership aren't there situations which he recognizes better than anyone else because of his over-all viewpoint? A strong yes can be the answer to both these questions, provided two pow-

---

[3] This is one of the most puzzling tendencies among educational people. To reject some idea as undesirable is one thing, but to assert its impossibility in the face of successful practice is a sad disavowal of the inquiring mind, the kind of mind which ought to be associated with education.

Another fascinating phenomenon is the prevailing tendency to refuse to assume responsibility. Administrators will say, "Teachers insist on this"; teachers will assert, "The administration requires it." Sometimes parents are brought into the act too.

erful controlling factors are taken into account. The first of these is timing. The principal may decide to defer mentioning a problem which unquestionably exists but has not crystallized enough for a good case to be made for its consideration. The situation might come under the heading of complacency, but it might be poor policy to make an issue of the problem *directly* at the moment.

The second controlling factor is the ability of the staff to weigh the principal's suggestions objectively along with the ideas presented by other staff members. If the principal's proposal for a problem is going to have precedence over the others, then there may not be many others because of a teacher's natural hesitancy to put his suggestion into competition with the favored proposal.

In other words, a principal should be very sure that his proposal amply justifies a favored position, one that will be generally recognized, before he makes his suggestion in a manner which may put others in a secondary light. Preferably, the principal ought to feel free to make any suggestions which will be evaluated on a basis of equality with suggestions from other faculty members.

The possibility of a problem emerging from faculty consideration which, in the principal's opinion, is most unwise must be pondered carefully before the proposal advances too far. It should not be advanced to the point of general faculty acceptance only to have the principal announce that the staff will not be permitted to pursue it. It would be much better for the principal to voice his misgivings when the proposal is first brought up. If he knows he must veto the idea, he should do so at the outset rather than mislead the staff into considering something which is impossible. Generally, a staff would recognize, if it had the information, the unsuitability of a proposal as well as a principal would. There could, however, be circumstances of a critical kind which the principal is not free to divulge. For example, there might be a touchy personnel situation, unknown to the staff in general, which would make it unwise to pursue a particular proposal. It is important, therefore, that any proposal which must be avoided should have its ultimate status made clear when it first arises. To do otherwise is to make foolishness out of the democratic process.

A faculty study problem should meet certain criteria if it is to be meaningful to a given school staff. Such criteria should be established by the faculty itself. The following are samples found in one school:

*1.* The problem should express a real concern of the teachers. School leaders in recent years have discovered that mere involvement of teachers in course of study development or similar production activities is no guarantee that what is developed will find its way into classroom use. School programs are changed only as teachers themselves change and grow.[4] Armstrong and Cushman state:

> Three principles of learning which are basic in an effective program of in-service education for teachers are: (*a*) learning takes place best when it begins with matters of real interest and concern to the learner; (*b*) the rate of learning is likely to increase as the area of his concern is extended; (*c*) continued learning is dependent upon the development of the individual's particular interests and potentialities.[5]

A similar opinion is expressed in *Schools for a New World:*

> Most rapid learning takes place when the learners—whether they be pupils, teachers, or parents—are attempting to achieve purposes that are significant to them at the time. A growing appreciation of this fact has caused many educators to change more or less radically their point of view toward in-service teacher education. The recent emphasis is to initiate a program of curriculum improvement by beginning with the specific and personal curriculum concerns of teachers. These are various and diverse. The theory is, first, that teachers are motivated to do constructive work if the work "makes sense" to them and, second, that no matter how peripheral or unique the curriculum problem may be, persistent and thoughtful work will inevitably lead to concern about more significant and central problems.[6]

*2.* A problem should hold forth some possibility of a solution or fruitful pursuit; in other words, it should not be so intangible

[4] George Sharp, *Curriculum Development as Re-education of the Teacher,* p. 2. New York: Bureau of Publications, Teachers College, Columbia, 1951.

[5] Department of Elementary School Principals, National Education Association, *In-service Growth of School Personnel,* Twenty-first Yearbook, p. 487. Washington, D. C.: The Department, 1942.

[6] American Association of School Administrators, *Schools for a New World,* Twenty-fifth Yearbook, pp. 144–45. Washington, D. C.: The Association, 1947.

or so overwhelming that nothing can be moved or changed. One way to see that a problem is kept within shooting range is to make it specific enough that definite outcomes or progress can be expected in at least a school year. "The high school curriculum" is a topic which might be studied for years without any particular effect on the school doing the studying. If, however, a faculty takes up the question, "Should we have social studies and English taught to the same pupils by the same teachers in the tenth grade next school year?" something is going to have to happen or good reasons given for its not happening.

3. Another important matter to consider is whether foundational work has been done in relation to a proposed curriculum study. If it is proposed that a high school build its program on a concept of adolescent needs, before an answer can be given agreement must be reached on just whose concept of adolescent needs is going to be employed. Some members of the staff, for instance, may firmly believe that the existing curriculum program very admirably meets these needs. Again, before a program is set up for gifted children, a decision will have to be reached on just who are the gifted ones and how many of them there are.

4. The problem and its possible answers or solutions should be consistent with the existing, emerging, or projected goals of the school system as well as the individual school. Sometimes, after a study has begun, faculties are surprised that they must make decisions they did not dream would come up when the study was first considered. Grouping of pupils, marking systems, honor societies, student councils, parent-teacher contacts, and courses of study are some of the areas of school life which in their present forms may be challenged as a curriculum study progresses. Unless a faculty really wants to see such areas of school life challenged, it should be careful to limit the scope of the study at the outset.

Deep in a study, system-wide, of the education of superior pupils, staff members of the Wilmington, Delaware, public schools were suddenly confronted with tentative conclusions in regard to the grouping of pupils which were at odds with the prevailing system-wide policy on grouping. They found it necessary not only

to re-think policy on grouping for superior pupils but also to consider basic educational philosophy in regard to goals and purposes
for *all* pupils. For a period of time it was necessary to ask individual school units to delay initiation of plans for dealing with
superior pupils until the conflicts in policy could be resolved.

Of course, what a member school does should fit into the over-
all pattern or philosophy of the whole school system. Even if
individual school units enjoy a high degree of autonomy, there
is still an obligation to see that a child's educational experiences,
as he moves upward through the school system, have some related-
ness in objective and outlook.

5. Certain areas of curriculum study have aspects on which
there can be a great deal of disagreement. The advisable degree
of pupil-teacher planning in a class is a question on which friend-
ships can cool; so is the question of evaluating pupil achievement.
There are teachers who firmly believe, if they've never had the
experience (and maybe if they have had), that a given class of
pupils simply cannot be held together, much less taught, more than
forty-five minutes at a time; these folk break out into a cold
sweat when the possibility of having a group of youngsters two
consecutive class periods is considered. These possible feelings of
staff members all point to the advisability of deciding, before a
curriculum project is launched, that pursuing the study will be
more unifying than divisive for the staff. If pursuit of the proposed project will mean violent battle, interdepartmental enmities,
and personal bitterness among the staff, should the study be followed at such a price?

On the other hand, the principal and faculty should make sure
that they are not frightened needlessly by a few excessively vocal
members whose influence is not in proportion to the volume of
their outcries. If the principal's leadership can tip the scales one
way or the other, then it definitely should be on the side which
will move the faculty forward. Curriculum study should not be
pursued at the price of disunity, but unity should not be pur-
chased at the lowest level of faculty outlook.

6. Since fear of community opposition, real or imagined, has

perhaps slowed down more curriculum advancement than any other factor, it might appear unnecessary to mention such a possibility as a criterion for choice of a problem. On the supposition, however, that not all schools have had the bitter community uprisings which some have experienced, it should be pointed out that community attitudes, even though not vocal at a given moment, do considerably modify what a school or school system may change or develop. Since in America the schools belong to the people, the people will help make educational decisions either in co-operation with professional educators or in opposition to them. This question ought to be looked at *before* a proposed study has been started rather than have it arise at a critical and embarrassing juncture later. The prevalence and the representativeness of any expression of community sentiment should be considered as well as the emphasis with which it is voiced. The mere presence in a community of a misunderstanding or of a critical attitude does not in itself excuse a faculty from studying its program. It is entirely possible that providing information and the opportunity for discussion of issues will enable a faculty to enlist the support of questioning community members. The essential point is that community attitude should be considered, not ignored or overlooked.

## Summary

The origin of problems, then, may be in these sources:

1. School-life activities
2. Previous staff study
3. Faculty census
4. Staff committees
5. System-wide leadership
6. In-service activities
7. Community pressures
8. Regional study groups
9. The principal

While every school staff ought to set up its own criteria for choice of a problem or a project, some critical questions relate to such matters as these:

1. Is the problem a real concern of the teachers?
2. Does it hold forth some hope of successful pursuit?

3. Has necessary foundational work been done on the problem?
4. Is the proposal consistent with school and school system policies and practices?
5. Will pursuit of the problem increase staff unity?
6. Will the proposal have community support?

Complete answers to these questions, of course, may not be available as a proposal is first contemplated. A tentative or trial working on the proposal may be advisable until enough information is gathered to justify a more organized formulation of the problem. In fact, more than one study proposal may be considered by the staff before a definite commitment is made to follow a particular one. As each tentative proposal is viewed in light of the faculty's criteria for formulating a problem, not only will a choice of an immediate problem be made but additional problems for future study may emerge.

*Chapter 4*

# HOW SHOULD THE PRINCIPAL AND STAFF ORGANIZE FOR WORK ON THE CURRICULUM PROBLEM?

HERE again, as in many other aspects of program planning, the principal and staff should follow their accustomed ways of working which they have found to be effective. A plan which may be workable in one school may be entirely unsuited for another. The suggestions concerning organization offered in this chapter are illustrative of plans which are known to have met with success in a specific situation.

In one medium-sized junior high school the faculty was organized into these committees: advisory, curriculum, professional, and pupil activities. In this school, matters dealing with curriculum were first discussed in the curriculum committee and then taken up with the faculty as a whole for final approval. In another medium-sized junior high school there was no curriculum committee as such; each grade level group of teachers did the curriculum planning for that grade level and the whole faculty took up curriculum issues of school-wide significance. In a large senior high school, curriculum problems were the province of the committee on philosophy and objectives. In such schools as these a standing committee can take the lead in developing a curriculum problem. A faculty would, in effect, say to this committee, "Bring us your findings and recommendations on the problem and we'll see what course we think we should follow. Meanwhile, keep us informed of your progress."

## A New Committee

There will be occasions when it is advisable to select a new working committee to tackle a study problem. A special working committee has the advantage of having a single task and perhaps personnel selected because of their interest or ability in regard to the problem under consideration. If the scope of the study problem warrants, either a standing committee or a special committee can be designated as a steering group, with subcommittees assuming responsibility for specialized jobs. A group of eighth grade teachers in one junior high school working on program changes for the following year set up this organization:

STAFF CURRICULUM COMMITTEE (STEERING)

SUBCOMMITTEES

| What pupils think about their needs. | What parents think about their children's needs. |
| What central office leaders think about pupil needs. | What the literature says about pupil needs. |

COMMITEE OF ALL EIGHTH GRADE TEACHERS

(To recommend changes in light of findings of above subcommittees)

When a curriculum study is quite extensive in scope, a staff may want to have standing committees proceed with the usual work of the faculty while the whole faculty is assigned to new groupings or subcommittees for the purpose of carrying on the study. One secondary school staff which had done a great deal of thinking on curriculum matters assigned all its teachers one year, in addition to their regular committee work, variously to four committees: Values, Nature of Learning, Reporting to Parents, Structure (Curriculum). These committees prepared written reports and, in addition, conducted faculty meetings built around committee findings and recommendations. Part of this organization carried over into the following school year, and for a period of five years the findings of the committees were focal points of reference in additional faculty study which led to further changes in the program.

## Communications Problems

The problem of how a curriculum study committee can keep in touch with the other members of the staff is one of the most challenging aspects of program improvement. It cannot be overemphasized, especially in large schools. Duplicated reports of findings and activities may give a feeling of accomplishment to committee members but have a dubious effect on other faculty members unless those teachers have some particular motive impelling them to read the reports. Oral reports may be of some help, but these too may be perfunctory and time-consuming. Perhaps the least appreciated method of all is to have someone at a meeting read a duplicated report, of which the members have copies in their hands.

Whatever the committee is reporting should answer a charge or commission given by the whole staff. Then there may be real concern about the committee's report. Also, more dramatic ways of presenting material than mere reciting may secure more interested attention. Role playing, well-planned conversation between two committee members, a debate of issues, questioning of a visiting consultant or of parents, use of charts and photographs are some of the possibilities. Another means of drawing teachers more actively into consideration of committee reports is to start a general staff meeting with a brief preview or summary of the issues and follow by breaking up into small discussion groups, each led by a committee member. Some faculties using this procedure have the discussion groups later report opinions back to the staff at large. The success of breaking the faculty into small discussion groups depends considerably upon the preparation and skill of members who preside over the discussions. After a faculty has had considerable experience with this technique, however, members may very well choose their own chairmen and recorders.

One variation of this plan of small discussion groups is to maintain the identity of the groups for the entire year and for all discussion purposes. This has the advantage of getting the members better acquainted and thus makes free discussion more likely. On the other hand, if the same discussion groups are to be used all year, they should be structured in membership so as to distribute the age groups, experience groups, departments, sex, and perhaps cliques.

## Problems of Flexibility

It has been pointed out that the staff at large should participate in setting up the goals and objectives for a committee's assignment, thus identifying the whole faculty with the project. If it is advisable to change, modify, or extend the goals and objectives during the progress of the study, the faculty should share in making these decisions; otherwise a committee may experience opposition among the faculty at a later date. While much helpful work can be accomplished, for instance, in a grade level group of teachers working intensively on a project concerned with that grade level, teachers in other grade levels, both preceding and following, will be affected by this work if it has any significance at all. If teachers in other grade levels do not understand and accept the particular study project, they may see their own security threatened as changes are made. Furthermore, in such a situation unwholesome competition can arise between teachers who are making changes and teachers who prefer the status quo. Such competition is perhaps natural when some classes of a certain grade level are following accustomed ways of working while other classes are changing patterns of work. If the faculty intend to study the differences in the two ways of working, as demonstrated by the two groups of classes, well and good; if, however, the faculty do not intend to make a comparison, then the situation may become rather difficult when the faculty at large has not accepted the goals of the group making the changes.

Unfortunately, pupils themselves may bear the brunt of unwholesome competition between teachers who are in a study project and teachers who oppose or have not accepted the purposes of the project. This can be especially troublesome if teachers not directly involved rightly or wrongly believe the pupils in the project to be privileged and favored. Similarly, difficulties may arise if non-involved teachers believe the pupils in a curriculum project are not achieving as well as they should in fundamental skills. Several pupils once told the writer that three years after they had been in an experimental class group they were still being reminded of it by a critical teacher when they missed a spelling word. Most of this trouble can be avoided when the whole faculty understands and accepts the goals of a committee or experimental group and thus is identified with the success of the committee's work. It is important to remember that this applies not only to the *initial* goals of a project but to the *changing* and *evolving* goals as well. As changed goals are indicated during the progress of a curriculum project, *all* the faculty should be informed of the need for change and should accept the particular revisions which are agreed upon.

## Research in Action

One means of keeping a curriculum study down to earth is to find ways of trying out some of the ideas considered, both the initial ideas and those which emerge in the study's progress, instead of just being content with talking about them. Action research done by other people may be of little moment to a teacher, but if this teacher discovers a certain truth in his own classroom experience, no matter how many people already know this truth, it can be very significant to him. Perhaps a committee is concerned with the possibility of an English teacher having the same group of pupils in both English and social studies. If Teacher Brown notices that he has Sections 10A and 10B in English and that Teacher Smith has the same sections in social studies, and he finds that Smith is willing to take Section 10B in both English and social studies while he does the same for Section 10A, then we have the makings of homemade experimentation.

When the spirit of adventure is present in a faculty it is not difficult to obtain volunteers for tryout experiences. The writer remembers visiting a ninth grade teachers' planning group in which shortly after one member proposed a certain change, three teachers indicated their willingness to try the change in their own classrooms before a final decision was made. In another school more teachers volunteered to work in "little school" groups than administrators could schedule the first year the plan was tried.[1] This is the typical way teachers respond when they are stimulated, encouraged, and supported.

Tryout experiences, too, can make achievement goals easier to attain and more exciting. Such goals should be set, in time and amount, for program improvement studies, lest months be consumed in nothing but talk. Even though these time marks may need to be changed later, they are helpful in keeping a staff moving toward specific attainments. Intermediate evaluation points can be set up for measuring progress against previously agreed upon goals. These goals themselves may need to be changed if the evaluation so indicates.

One of the signs of a mature faculty is its ability to abandon failures and unwise procedures without a feeling of defeat. Sometimes plans which, from all appearances, ought to work, and have worked in other schools, just don't pan out. In such a situation a staff should either modify the plan so it does work in that school or abandon the plan in favor of something which is more usable. This is another argument for tryout experiences early in the development of a curriculum study before a staff has become so involved and committed that a change of plans is costly and difficult.

## Faculty Conference Groups

Staff conference groups which meet weekly or biweekly during unassigned class periods of teachers provide machinery for more intensive faculty study than is usually possible in large staff meetings. These are some advantages of this way of working:

1. Frequency of the meetings makes for more continuity.
2. Membership in the groups may cut across department lines and thus ensure a wider exchange of thinking.

[1] For discussion of "little school" groups, see pp. 73–75.

3. Meetings are relatively brief, since they must be confined to a class period.
4. If membership in each group is kept to ten or so as a maximum, everyone on the faculty will have, in the run of the school year, an opportunity to present his views.
5. Since the groups are small, parents who are invited will feel much freer to participate.
6. These groups meet during the school day and therefore can be considered a part of the regular work load.
7. The small size of the groups permits more informal meetings; many such groups will enjoy including coffee on the agenda.

These are some of the disadvantages of this way of working:

1. Some teachers may feel one of their "free" periods has been taken away. This feeling is not likely to arise if holding conference groups at unassigned periods tends to decrease the number of after-school meetings teachers are expected to attend. Also, this disadvantage will be at a minimum as teachers find that they are talking about matters of interest to them and that their opinions have weight.
2. Communication among the groups and with the faculty at large will still be a problem. Faculty meetings could be used to summarize developments in the various groups. Another possibility is for an over-all conference committee, with representatives from each conference group, to assume responsibility for hearing progress reports and informing the various groups about them. Since each member of such a conference committee would also be a member of an individual conference discussion group, the communication between the over-all committee and the groups should not be difficult.
3. Leadership may be hard pressed to keep up with all the groups, especially in a large school. Yet such groups offer the principal an effective channel of two-way communication with his staff.

The school problems listed on pages 21, 22, and 23 were suggested in such conference groups and much of the follow-up work was carried on with the same organization.

### Role of Subject Departments

What part should subject area departments play in organization for curriculum study? The answer to this question depends, in part, on how thoroughly the school is departmentalized. If the thinking and planning of the staff have been for years directed through the departments, it may be difficult at first to get teachers to work understandingly with members of other departments. The department chairman, of course, occupies a key position in this respect. If the various department chairmen work well together and are not particularly jealous of each other's privileges, it is likely that other members of the departments will work co-operatively. The principal is also a key person in the question of interdepartmental planning. If in frequent meetings with department chairmen he encourages a concept of school-wide outlook, the chairmen will reflect some of this attitude in their dealings within their departments.

As curriculum studies progress one frequent difficulty is that department chairmen may see their security threatened in new curriculum organizations which combine subject areas or which require close co-operation of people in different departments. Similarly, teachers in the departments may feel that such plans as unified studies unjustly require the teachers to teach subjects they do not prefer or for which they are not qualified.

Such problems will require a great deal of patience and understanding on the part of the principal. In some cases he may even have to defer certain plans and developments because of the obstinacy or sincere opposition on the part of a department chairman or even an entire department. It is a questionable procedure to force a staff member, especially one in leadership such as a department chairman, into a course which he deeply abhors. On a practical basis, it may mean that certain subject departments in a school will forge ahead of others. The problem of what to do with an eager and co-operative teacher who is a member of a department whose chairman disagrees with what the school is trying to accomplish will tax the ingenuity of the principal who wants to be fair to everybody. One possibility is to transfer the teacher to another department in which he can participate in curriculum study, but it would tend further to isolate the reluctant chairman's department from the life stream of the school if only teachers who are content to refrain from staff studies are assigned to the department. It must not be forgotten that superintendents sometimes have similar problems with principals who resist curriculum change. A reluctant principal can hold back a whole staff; a reluctant chairman can hold back his department.

Fortunately, certain types of curriculum study do not threaten departmental lines, in fact, may give one department the lead, yet afford others the opportunity of participation. How to improve school citizenship is a project in which the social studies department might take the lead but all departments would have a share. How to improve written communication might be the first job of the English department but all departments would have a stake in its success. The possibility of asking one of the department chairmen to head up such a study for the entire faculty should not be overlooked.

### Staff Structure

If there is too much resistance to change in the departmental organization itself and it appears that to await personnel changes would be an unjustifiable delay, then perhaps the principal and staff should consider new staff structure to make program change more likely. Even when departmental leaders are co-operative, some thought might well be given to further staff organization which may make curriculum change more efficient. School-wide committees on citizenship, development of responsibility, use of community resources, techniques of teacher-pupil planning, preparation of resource units, and other aspects of the instructional life of the school may assist teachers in any or all subject areas to carry out agreed upon changes. Appointment of grade level chairmen and the establishment of "little schools" are other possibilities.[2]

Another approach is to set up a new staff position of curriculum

[2] For a discussion of "little schools," see pages 73–75.

assistant or vice-principal in charge of curriculum planning.[3] This person would be available to help all teachers with problems of instruction and planning. The question of staff acceptance of this individual, especially if the outward framework of departmental organization is maintained, would need to be considered carefully.[4] If department chairmen are reluctant to co-operate with the principal in bringing about change, they are more than likely to be reluctant to co-operate with a curriculum assistant. It is important to define carefully the role of the new staff member and his relationship to the existing faculty organization. In no case should the principal and the superintendent try to escape their leadership responsibility by setting up new positions to deal with curriculum problems. New personnel may bring greater dispatch and effectiveness to the program but they cannot relieve the principal and the superintendent from *their* responsibility.

## Summary

This chapter has set forth the following considerations in regard to organizing the staff for work on a curriculum problem:

*1.* Organization for working on a problem should fit the needs and accustomed ways of working of the particular staff.

*2.* Special committees for a project can give it concentrated attention.

[3] Departmental problems aside, such a staff person can perform valuable service in assisting new and probationary teachers with their problems of planning and classroom management.

Each high school in Portland, Oregon, has three vice-principals of equal status, one of whom is responsible for program planning under the guidance of the principal. The other two vice-principals deal with pupil problems, and in addition there is an activities director. Each faculty has a curriculum committee with which the vice-principal in charge of curriculum planning works. This committee meets weekly to consider suggestions from individual teachers and from the subject departments as well as from committee members.

[4] The writer remembers how dismayed he and some other principals were a few years ago over staff resistance to a new position which the principals had persuaded the superintendent to set up in each school. The two years of resistance to the new curriculum worker would have been better spent *before* the appointment in planning with the faculty on staff needs in this area of program planning.

3. Communication between project committees and staff must be safeguarded.

4. The staff at large should share in establishing original and changing goals.

5. The study problem should include provision for early try-out experiences by willing teachers.

6. Achievement and time goals should be set up even though they may have to be modified later.

7. Failures should be recognized and plans changed accordingly.

8. Conference groups that meet weekly or biweekly during unassigned class periods of teachers have certain advantages.

9. Subject departments, if their leaders are willing, should be brought into the study.

10. Staff committees or grade level chairmen might provide supplementary leadership when departmental organization is reluctant to provide for it.

11. Appointment of a curriculum assistant or vice-principal in charge of curriculum planning could aid the principal in leadership of curriculum study.

Whatever organization is agreed upon for curriculum study, it is important as soon as it can be carried out to involve in-the-classroom experiences and findings of teachers. As is suggested in this chapter, experimentation should be an integral part of program improvement.[5] Thus, ideas are put to the practical test as a study progresses, and the study then is kept within the confines of the possible and the desirable.

[5] Experimentation as used throughout this monograph does not necessarily imply traditional formal research; rather the term refers to tryout experiences that are appropriate to many areas of school activity.

# Chapter 5

# WHAT RESOURCES ARE AVAILABLE TO THE PRINCIPAL AND STAFF AS THEY PLAN FOR PROGRAM IMPROVEMENT?

Full utilization should be made of system-wide leadership. It has already been suggested that if opposition to a proposed staff study is expected from central leadership, then the advisability of beginning the study at all is a serious question. On the other hand, it is quite possible for central office leadership to look favorably upon a staff project and yet not be given any opportunity to participate. Those in supervisory positions can be of practically no use to a staff unless they are made welcome in the school unit. The person, of course, who must take the lead in maintaining a pleasant, cooperative relationship between the school staff and central office leadership is the principal.

Supervisors and other central staff personnel can be of assistance in virtually every phase of a study problem's development. Naturally they are going to be of limited help if they are kept only on the periphery of a problem. They ought to be attached to actual working committees and the other on-going activities pertaining to the problem's development. This is not only for the help they can give the staff, but for their own help in keeping in touch with teachers' problems and in understanding teachers more fully. Preferably the supervisor should work in a teacher group as a resource person and as a group participant rather than as director of the group. In some situations a supervisor's specialty or subject competence can be utilized to advantage. One curriculum director, for instance, has a major interest in science and unusual competence in industrial arts. He has given direct and practical assistance to many teachers who are planning work alcoves for their classrooms.

It is to be hoped that system-wide personnel will not make the error of assuming an unduly critical attitude toward staff members who are to be helped. At best, it is tempting for classroom teachers to think that persons who have been out of the classroom for many years tend to offer suggestions which would not be made by a person who had to carry them out. If to this is linked a tendency to "tell them," the usefulness of a system-wide person may be limited.

The writer remembers a painful history department meeting in which the members were attempting to revise the course outlines then in use. A consultant from the central office was convinced that the history teachers should, instead, be reorganizing their whole concept of course content and ways of working. He was frank enough to say so. He persisted in maintaining this viewpoint in the face of determined resistance on the part of the department members. Finally one teacher frostily inquired if the consultant was really acquainted with the everyday problems of teaching history. The consultant stated he had spent many years in the classroom and was well acquainted with its problems. "How many years ago was that?" demanded another member of the department, and it was as though every teacher in the room had helped make this telling thrust. The consultant's usefulness to the history department came to a speedy end. If this system-wide leader had been content to help these teachers with the problem they were diligently working on, he might later have assisted them along the lines he had in mind.

While it may be true that some principals have not been very active in stirring lethargic teachers, it is also possible that system-wide leaders would be just as inactive if they had to work with the teachers in question on a day-to-day basis. Surely the lethargic teachers and the indiscreet supervisors and directors are in the minority. Possible friction or misunderstanding will be greatly reduced if the principal will take at least two precautions. One is to talk over problems with the system-wide leader in advance of a meeting and the other is to be present at the meeting. The ideal situation is one in which the supervisor or director is a partner in leadership with the principal.

Counsel between system-wide personnel and a school principal should, of course, be two-way. Just as a principal should talk over plans with the appropriate central office person, members of the central office should in turn make it a point to inform school principals of policies which are evolving and changing for the system as a whole. While it is advisable for principals to share in developing system-wide policies, it is not expedient to have them spend much of their time in the central office. When principals are invited to share in system-wide planning, they should not be brought in unprepared, any more than a supervisor or other central personnel should be thrust into a faculty meeting without prior orientation. In either case adequate background preparation will enhance the possibility of mutual understanding and thus of group progress. In some school systems central personnel set up system-wide policy meetings in various school building units instead of arranging for all important sessions to be held in the central headquarters.

The system-wide staff member can also be of aid in relating a given school's study to those of other schools in the system. This point is more pertinent perhaps in the large school systems having two or more school units at the same level; however, it is also applicable in the small school system because of the need to relate elementary school studies to those of the secondary school. Such problems as reporting pupil progress, fundamental purposes of school, the science program, parent contacts, and child development are of common concern in all branches of a school system. A school staff should profit from a study similar to its own being carried on in a neighbor school; also, in the system at large an effort should be made to keep staff studies consistent with school system practices. The central staff leader should share in this responsibility.

### Inter-School Study

How important is this problem? First, for different school units at the same level, such as two senior high schools, there is the problem of transfer of pupils from one school to the other. If the programs of the two schools are entirely independent of each other, pupils and their parents may have difficulty in adjusting to the differences. This is not to say that all units of a school system should proceed in lock step; but at least they should not set forth in opposite directions! Obviously, it is appropriate for a given school to try certain arrangements or experiences not being carried on by other schools in the system. It should be just as obvious that if two or more schools are launching similar studies, they can learn from each other's activities.

Some thought ought to be given, too, to what is done to pupils when one school initiates curricular changes irrespective of other school units in the system. For example, if a high degree of pupil-teacher planning is followed in one school but is not encouraged in another school, pupils will have difficulty adjusting from one to the other if they transfer. It may be argued that if a pupil moves out of a community he has to adjust to whatever new school situation he finds, but this is no justification for school staffs in the same school system not to be concerned about what each other is doing.

It is true that pupils, like other people, can adjust to almost anything if they have to, even conflicting philosophy and practices. But is this the most efficient learning experience the school system can provide? Is it possible that having special classes for slow learners in elementary schools and the senior high school but not in the junior high school, all in the same school system, is carrying school autonomy too far? Is it wise to teach pupils in one grade level how to work together toward goals which they help set up only to have them told the following year that they are not old enough to help set up their own goals and must take what is set before them? Vertical articulation in a school system is important to the child. Even if he is expected to adjust to differences in outlook and methods, he still has the right to careful orientation from one unit to another, and for this reason alone, if for no other, the school staffs concerned should know what each is doing. Such considerations make it imperative for a principal and his staff to ponder carefully the effect of a proposed change on other schools in the system. The central staff's resources should be brought to bear on the problem.

One way of getting inter-school thinking on program improvement is to invite advisory groups of staff members from other schools to sit in on certain stages of the planning. These folk then would be informed of what is taking place and would have an opportunity to exert influence if they feel some unwise procedure is being proposed. Furthermore, they could take back to their own schools promising developments which they observe. If the visiting advisory group comes from a school which has had experiences similar to the ones being contemplated, then this group can share those experiences for what they are worth.

Elementary school teachers not only will be interested in the orientation aspect of changes in a high school's program but will be concerned also about how they can contribute toward the high school's goals in their own instructional program. This is assuming, of course, that the elementary school teachers and the high school teachers are on good terms and are not blaming each other for all the ills of society. Secondary school teachers can learn much from elementary school teachers about the particular children who are moving into the secondary school and about the experiences they have had which can be built upon in the high school.

In the event that two or more schools in the same system are working on similar curriculum studies simultaneously, they could have a joint committee for consultation and their staffs could arrange for intervisitation in classrooms and other school activities involved. There could even be situations in which pupils from each school work together in a joint enterprise, such as a community survey.

Existing system-wide committees offer another channel for

inter-school communication on curriculum study. This is especially true if there is a system-wide curriculum committee charged with the responsibility of general oversight of curriculum studies in the system. Then too, system-wide meetings of principals and supervisors will afford opportunity for an exchange of information relative to program changes under consideration. Supervisors and directors of instruction will be in a position to coordinate developments in the various schools and to assist in the exchange of information.

The right of school staffs to forge ahead ought to be safe-guarded. Their obligation to keep in touch with each other ought to be observed.

## Help from Outside

In this day of swift and distant commuting, almost any school is within reach of college and university staff services. Some of these services, like those of the Horace Mann-Lincoln Institute of Teachers College, Columbia University, are extended to affiliated school systems over a period of years; others are offered in terms of a particular job to be done in a specified interval of time. College and university staff services cannot furnish easy, quick answers to a school system's problems. They can, however, assist schools and school systems in working toward their own answers to their own problems. Obviously, to bring in an outside consultant for one lecture or for even one session with a committee has very limited effectiveness. It is much more fruitful to establish a continuing consultantship or service which will give the consultant an opportunity to get acquainted with the school or school system and thus be in a position to offer real assistance.

If, however, it is possible to have a consultant for only one session or for a very brief time—and this is probably better than no consultant at all—his effectiveness can be increased by furnishing him advance summaries of progress, along with issues on which his reaction will be appreciated. Furthermore, he may be able to take with him, from the conference, certain materials which he can react to and return with suggestions at a later date. If it is the consultant's first visit in the community, advance information about community characteristics would be of help to him. Also, a visiting consultant should not be expected to pull local chestnuts out of the fire, especially if he has not been informed about them. One consultant was asked what appeared to be an innocent question on the maximum desirable enrollment for a junior high school. The next thing he knew, he was in the middle of a local argument over the size of the proposed junior high school and, to his embarrassment, was asked to explain why his suggested maximum enrollment was so different from that of another consultant.

The experiences of other school systems in similar projects may be of guidance. Some of these experiences are reported in educational journals and one can write to the principals of the schools in question for further information. If the resources of the home school system permit, a staff member from the school system which is carrying on interesting projects relating to the local one may be invited in as a consultant. Sometimes he can be persuaded to drop off for an extra day on his return from a national convention, if the inviting school system is in a convenient location.

In other circumstances the home school system may find it expedient to have several of its staff members visit the school system carrying on the practice in which the home system is interested. This has the advantage that the staff members get to see the practice in actual operation and can talk with teachers responsible at the operational level. It is much better for visiting teachers to participate in and observe the actual on-going activities of a project than to have extensive formal conferences "about the project." An introductory background conference is advisable, yes, but an opportunity ought to be presented for visiting teachers to see the program in action.[1]

Another source of clues regarding schools carrying on interesting practices is the staffs of colleges and universities who hear

[1] Visits from personnel of other school systems can, of course, be quite a problem to school systems carrying on well-publicized projects. It has been necessary for some school systems to limit the number of visitors and to schedule their visits so as not to interfere with the work of pupils and teachers.

of these practices from their students and from their own consultant activities.

Outcomes other than information relating to specific projects in other school systems can emerge from visits. General organization, administration, and programs of other schools are usually of interest to visiting teachers. Some school systems set aside one work day in the school year for faculties to visit in other school districts. Frequently teachers who attend conventions and conferences are asked by their faculty or principal to visit schools which are in session in the convention city. Visiting in another school can be a very worth-while source of new ideas if the venture is carefully planned and the information obtained is evaluated. The faculty in one large school planned its day of visits in twenty-three schools of the surrounding region by preparing a check list of items which were to be studied. Copies of the check list were sent ahead to the schools to be visited. After the faculty members returned from their visits, they gave the information they had gathered to the vice-principal, who compiled a summary of the data. These data included size of schools, length of school day, number of class periods per week, length of class periods, use of the activity period, faculty organization, curriculum organization, extra pay for extra work, and departmental organization. The faculty then had much interesting and useful information for its own committees which were studying some of the items listed.

There are times, of course, when teachers or others who have misgivings about certain school practices, proposed or in effect, are encouraged by knowing that other schools are following similar procedures. Also, teachers, either through visitation or from written inquiry, may discover new practices in other schools which they may want to consider for their own. When it is impossible to make a direct staff-to-staff contact with another school system in regard to an interesting practice, some information may be obtained from correspondence. This, of course, has limited possibilities if a particular school system is deluged with inquiries. Sometimes teachers or committees try to get desired information by sending multiple inquiries to many school systems. Justification of existing or proposed procedures, however, by the mere counting of schools employing them is open to question. Situations which prevail in the other schools may not be present in the local setup. Differences in community structure, in characteristics of population, in professional outlook, and in financial resources may distinguish what one school should do from what others are doing.

## Professional Literature

Another resource in curriculum study is professional books and journals. Here again, applicability to the local situation must be kept in mind. Teachers who are accustomed to having professional books and journals readily available make good use of them when a particular problem on which they want help arises. In fact, in the school which has a good professional bookshelf, teachers will get help in discovering and formulating problems as well as help toward their solution.

Books such as Alberty's *Reorganizing the High School Curriculum*,[2] Caswell's *The American High School*,[3] and Leonard's *Developing the Secondary School Curriculum*[4] provide general background information on the philosophy and structure of the high school curriculum. There are many others, not only in this field but also on public school curriculum theory and practice, philosophical foundations, techniques of group planning, and psychology of learning which a principal will want to make available to his teachers. If there are no curriculum books or readings on the school's "professional" shelf, the principal or teacher committee will be able to locate standard texts on secondary school administration which include chapters and bibliographies on curriculum.[5]

[2] Harold Alberty, *Reorganizing the High School Curriculum*. New York: The Macmillan Company, 1950.
[3] Hollis L. Caswell, *The American High School*. New York: Harper and Brothers, 1945.
[4] J. Paul Leonard, *Developing the Secondary School Curriculum*. New York: Rinehart and Company, 1946.
[5] Such as J. B. Edmonson, Joseph Roemer, and Francis L. Bacon, *The Administration of the Modern Secondary School*. New York: The Macmillan Company, 1953. Also Will French, J. Dan Hull, and B. L. Dodds, *American High School Administration: Policy and Practice*. New York: Rinehart and Company, 1951.

Some materials, such as the yearbooks of the Association for Supervision and Curriculum Development[6] and the *Bulletin* of the National Association of Secondary-School Principals,[7] present extensive discussions on issues and techniques in curriculum planning. Several of the Association for Supervision and Curriculum Development yearbooks provide excellent and rather complete descriptions of newer practices in various communities. Certain numbers of the N.A.S.S.P. *Bulletin* have been built around particular secondary school functions or issues. Some of the subject area groups, for example, the National Council of Teachers of English, National Council for the Social Studies, and National Council for the Teachers of Science, have produced material in recent years which ought to be of help in curriculum studies.[8] Regular issues of *Educational Leadership, The Clearing House, The School Executive, The Nation's Schools,* the *N.E.A. Journal, Teachers College Record,* and other professional magazines frequently have articles dealing with program improvement. It is not the purpose here to suggest a complete professional library; however, it might be said in passing that there is justification for including some general magazines as well as professional for teachers to use in the study of program improvement, especially from the standpoint of helping them study American thought and traditions. Then, too, the general magazines have provided a good deal of counsel on educational matters in the past few years.

Some school systems have sent teachers to summer school for study of a problem or project of interest to the local system. Occasionally teachers are sent in groups and receive special help on their school system's problems. When they return, they may work directly on the problem and they may also become resource lead-

[6] Such as Association for Supervision and Curriculum Development, N.E.A., *Action for Curriculum Improvement,* 1951 Yearbook. Washington, D. C.: The Association.

[7] Such as National Association of Secondary-School Principals, "Improving Instruction in the Secondary Schools," *The Bulletin,* Vol. 39, November, 1955.

[8] See, for example: George L. Fersh, editor, *The Problems Approach and the Social Studies.* Washington, D. C.: National Council for the Social Studies, 1955.

ers for other teachers. Several colleges and universities have set up campus workshops centering on problems of concern to the member students These workshops enable the teachers attending them to concentrate in small and intensive groups; social activities are often included as well as work sessions.

Local workshops, sponsored by university or college and carrying graduate credit, are about the ultimate in convenience for teachers, especially teachers who because of personal problems cannot travel to a distant campus. Furthermore, a workshop at home base makes it possible to call in administrative staff and other resource people from the school system for occasional conferences. The Springfield, Missouri, school system, which conducted seven summer workshops between 1942 and 1951, always included one or two local school system leaders on the staff, other workshop staff members being from the sponsoring university.[9] Inviting community members to appear on panels and as discussion participants was another feature of these workshops. Six of the seven workshops carried graduate credit, and attendance at any of them qualified a teacher to meet the school system's requirement that each teacher earn five graduate credits every five years in order to advance on the salary schedule.

Each Springfield workshop was planned by a teacher committee which not only recruited the workshop members but also polled them for problems and from these problems set up the working groups. The committee also consulted with the sponsoring university in choosing the workshop staff and in setting up the workshop machinery.

Other school systems have administered a different type of workshop which meets weekly for two or more hours at a time during the school year. Such a plan usually deals with a specific school problem or subject area and may or may not carry graduate credit, depending on the sponsoring university or college. The instructor or leader is usually furnished by the sponsoring institution, though in some cases he may be a member of the local school

[9] Two of these workshops were sponsored by Northwestern, one by Columbia, three by New York University, and one was sponsored locally.

system. In this type of workshop an entire faculty may constitute a workshop group or the workshop may be recruited from many different faculties in the school system.

Another type of resource is one which a staff may itself develop concurrently with the progress of a project for curriculum improvement. This includes minutes of meetings, plans agreed upon, outlines, guides, and lists of materials. While it is generally believed that the major benefit in developing resource materials comes to the persons preparing them, there is another group of teachers—teachers new to the school system—who stand to gain a great deal from having such records available. Even those who have been in the curriculum project from its beginning will find that minutes and reports of earlier stages of development are helpful in evaluation as well as in providing guides to next steps.

Some state departments of instruction and county superintendents' offices provide advisory services for schools and school systems whose staffs are considering curriculum study. A school staff should certainly take advantage of help from such agencies when possible. If the particular secondary school is located in a state in which there is considerable state-wide standardization of curriculum structure, the school staff will of necessity consult with the state department of instruction before making changes in curriculum structure. Even when this is not the case, it is advisable for a principal to check with his state department of instruction to see if school curriculum consultant services are provided. The same would be true, of course, of a county superintendent's office for schools under the direction of a county superintendent.

## Summary

In this chapter these resources have been discussed:

1. System-wide leadership.
2. Planning with other schools in the same system.
3. Consultant services.
4. Studying practices of schools in other communities.

5. Professional books and journals.
6. Specific studies in summer school at colleges and universities.
7. Local workshops.
8. Curriculum project records.
9. State or county departments of instruction.

Whatever resources or combinations of resources are employed, the main impetus and sense of direction should come from within the staff itself. There are no resources more powerful than the staff's and principal's willingness to move ahead and their skill in working together.

# Chapter 6

# HOW CAN THE PRINCIPAL AND STAFF INCLUDE
# PARENTS IN CURRICULUM PLANNING?

SOME co-operative experience with the school staff should precede parents' involvement in curriculum problems. There are many operational problems on which parents and teachers can learn to work together. Arranging for transportation on field trips, helping with costumes for a special assembly, sharing as hosts to a student council convention, serving as chaperons at school parties, assisting the staff at athletic contests, working with teachers at the educational exhibit in the county fair are some of the means through which parents have been brought into school life. The writer hesitates to mention money-raising activities for he believes parents have been asked to do too much along this line; however, it must be acknowledged that many stage curtains, office duplicating machines, school motion picture projectors, and even draperies in principals' offices attest to the hard-working and enthusiastic support which parent groups give to schools throughout the nation.

It is not suggested here that parents' activities be confined to a school's operational problems. The point is that parents and teachers ought to begin their working relationships with relatively non-controversial projects before the complex problems of school curriculum are taken up. When it is realized that some high school principals do not believe in parent participation in school policy making, and, in fact, will not permit parent-teacher groups to be affiliated with their schools, it will be seen that parents cannot be catapulted into the mysteries of curriculum planning. If a new principal moves into a situation in which parents have not been permitted to share in school life activities at all, he should work toward building a good co-operative relationship with parents before he asks them to delve into complex school issues on which not even school people are in complete agreement.

Co-operation with parent groups pays dividends if school people will invest a little confidence. Curriculum change, if it has any significance at all, is going to be of interest and concern to parents and other members of the community. It may be that school people who do not view parents as partners in developing school policy will not have a broad enough outlook on curriculum to want to change it anyway!

It can truly be said that no more important aspect of school-home co-operation will be discovered than that of curriculum planning. The fundamental belief in our nation that much of the basic control of schools should be vested in local communities makes it incumbent upon school leaders to develop that kind of school program which expresses the highest aspirations of the people whose children are served. It follows that school leaders must learn what these aspirations are, and what better way to find out than to ask the people themselves?

Assuming some background of school-parent co-operation, early involvement of parents in study programs will encourage their support. This will be no problem if the school is already accustomed to including parents in the planning activities of the staff. For schools where this has not been the custom, it may take some time for teachers and parents to feel at ease working together.

If a parent-teacher or home and school organization already exists, leaders in that group can be trained as discussion leaders. It should be made clear at the outset that parent discussion groups are not legislative; it can be pointed out that teachers themselves have not drawn conclusions on the matters being considered. On the other hand, members in a discussion group should be encouraged to make suggestions, to raise questions, and to pose problems. Thought ought to be given to what the leader should do if a member of a discussion group tries to monopolize the discussion or inject unrelated or highly questionable issues. Discussion leaders can be trained to handle such situations fairly to all, but if no thought has been given to the possibility, embarrassing predicaments can arise.

What is the role of teachers in discussion groups? (We're still talking of situations in which there has not been extensive participation by parents in school policy discussion.) If teachers fear they are going to be put on the defensive in a parent discussion, they are certainly going to be reluctant to take part. If there is any point at which it is justifiable to ask the mature, experienced teachers to take the lead, this is certainly one. If it is feared that critical questions will arise, teachers should consider who should meet such questions and how. The role of the teacher in a parent discussion group is to provide necessary background information to help parents understand the issues and problems. It is to encourage questions and comments; it is not to monopolize the situation nor to assume the defensive.

The principal and staff will be exercising good judgment in establishing initial parent discussion groups around topics or problems which are not likely to invite excessive controversy or displays of personality. After such a group has gotten well acquainted and has taken on some of the characteristics of group maturity, there will be time to take up more difficult issues.

This is another argument, of course, for involving parents early in the progress of a curriculum study rather than bringing them in later to be "reported to," only to find that some serious parent opposition threatens success of the enterprise. If it develops that a community will not accept or support a particular idea or plan, the sooner the school people discover this fact and take it into account, the better off everyone will be.

On the other hand, some issues, if looked at frankly and thoroughly early in a study, may be resolved to the complete satisfaction of parents and thus make likely their acceptance. This assumes, moreover, that school people are capable of modifying their position in light of dominant community sentiment and will not insist on the establishment of their desires or plans at all costs.

In other words, as a parent-teacher discussion group demonstrates its ability to cope with issues frankly and fairly, it should be given the opportunity to do so.

Actually, parents are just as eager for a discussion group to succeed as teachers are. For every parent who is inclined to be aggressive in meetings there may be five others who, if left alone, will sit through an entire meeting without any overt response. To get the thinking of *all*, not just that of the ready ones, is the challenge in a parents' meeting. As group members realize that school people are sincere in their quest for parent thinking, real power will emerge that is even greater than the power of groups that have achieved through negative attacks a part in school policy making. Why not mobilize this power to move the school's program forward instead of back?

## Group Size

Another question relating to discussion groups is that of size. While some ideas can be presented adequately in an auditorium-size gathering, the direction of communication is largely one-way. Extensive participation by individuals means that some plan of smaller groups will have to be put into effect. Actually, both the large audience and the small groupings can be employed in the same evening. Introductory explanations are presented in the large meeting and then smaller groups form to discuss the issues. Either all the groups may discuss the same list of issues or only one or two issues may be discussed in a group, members in each group being recruited on the basis of their interest in the issues on the agenda of that group.

The Upper Darby, Pennsylvania, Junior High School set up its parent discussion of school issues by drawing its leaders from a group of parents trained by other parents who had attended extension classes in group dynamics. In order not to start too ambitiously, the leaders decided to set up the first discussion meeting in one grade level only. A tryout experience was arranged with the homeroom mothers group; here topics for the large meeting were proposed and adopted. On the evening for the grade level discussions all participants met in the auditorium for orientation and then, after the small group discussions, returned to the auditorium for reports.

A large senior high school, faced with the problem of parents not feeling at ease in large parent-teacher meetings, arranged a series of meetings in elementary school buildings where senior high teachers discussed school problems with high school parents living in the vicinity.

In another senior high school several years ago the parents decided to replace the conventional P.T.A. organization with a parent advisory conference composed of some twenty representatives who met monthly with high school leaders to discuss problems of school program. Parent members of this conference were nominated by high school subject area departments.

A medium-sized junior high school's staff persuaded its P.T.A. to limit its large meetings to three for the school year. For the other months discussion meetings were held in the homes of volunteer parents in representative sections of the district. These parent hosts invited other parents in their neighborhoods into their homes for the discussions. The school staff was distributed, three or four teachers to each home, among the various meetings. Topics for discussion were planned by a joint parent-teacher committee from problems suggested by parents.

Some school faculties invite representative parents to sit in on regular staff committees. The number of parents who can do so is, of course, limited. If, however, the parents who attend staff committee meetings have the time to do so on a continuing basis, they are in a position to make a real contribution. To what extent they represent the thinking of parents who are not privileged to attend, it is difficult to say. If, however, the faculty is organized into working committees dealing with a rather comprehensive curriculum study, enough parents might be secured to work with these various committees and in turn become discussion leaders in parent groups, thus aiding in communication between staff and community members.

Many faculties prefer to call in parents only at certain intervals for progress reports. Parents may be organized as an advisory group and may even represent certain organized groups, such as civic clubs. It is hoped that representatives from various agencies would not look upon themselves as official representatives and go back to their groups for votes on certain issues. Such votes would depend upon the interpretation of the particular representative and could be the source of difficulty. It would be much better for the staff to see that an advisory group of parents is representative in the sense that a wide range of interests is present rather than to have the parents represent definite community agencies. To avoid appearing to select only its favorites for a parent advisory group, the faculty might ask a committee of community leaders to suggest members.

Parents, of course, could simply be invited to an open meeting to hear progress reports. This would avoid some of the difficulties of deciding who is representing whom, but it might also lay the meeting open to packing by a pressure group if there is some controversy between the school and any community group. Each principal and staff will have to know their community and the most desirable procedure to follow.

It should be said again that it would be much better to bring parents into curriculum studies early so that possible issues and controversies can be looked at candidly long before the school stakes its community support on any particular position. Whatever means is used to recruit parents, there should be provision for finding out what they think. Parents should be more than mere listening panels if their support of the school's program is to be substantial. Questions should be encouraged and should be answered. Opposition should not be beaten down; it should be convinced or the staff should take a fresh look at the school's position.

## Communications and the Community

The school can take its story directly into the community through news media, public relations programs, and direct contacts with community groups. Direct contacts may be occasions when the principal or other staff members speak to civic clubs and other community agencies. Such gatherings would obviously be unofficial so far as the school is concerned, although there may be club members who expect the school principal to speak with the voice of authority and thus answer their questions with finality. Experienced principals are accustomed to this risk and in most situations will meet it satisfactorily.

In addition to distributing its school newspaper to pupils, Reed Junior High School in Springfield, Missouri, mails it to every home in the district. This school paper has one page of material written by parents. Lower Merion Township, Pennsylvania, school system devotes one page of its staff newspaper to articles by and for parents. The Wilmington, Delaware, school system publishes a monthly journal, *Our Schools,* addressed to parents and community. Many other school systems follow similar practices to inform their communities of school events and school developments.

Certain school systems with active public relations departments have established rather extensive and continuing contacts with their communities through press releases, radio programs, and television programs. Each school in the system may be given its turn to produce a program on some phase of school life. Much co-operative planning and significant activity can go into such experiences. The school band, the safety club, the dramatics class, or a discussion by social studies students may help portray the school in a favorable light via radio or television.

These portrayals, excellent though they may be, are not sufficient communication between school and community for the consideration of curriculum change. They are by nature one-way communication and emphasize the dramatic and show-worthy. Then too, the technical requirements for programing impose certain restrictions on participants, materials, location, and scope which tend to modify considerably the characteristics of a school life activity from its natural setting and time sequence. This is not an argument against school radio and television productions, for these programs can have a powerful and positive influence on a community's attitude toward its schools. It is an argument, however, for a principal and faculty not to be content with such productions. In addition, lines of communication need to be established which will enable the school staff to *exchange* ideas with parents, not just *present* ideas. Newspaper articles, contacts with civic groups, and radio and television productions are important means of communication between school and community, but other means of communication will have to be provided if there is to be real exchange of ideas.

In curriculum changes which involve the question of community support, the board of education should not be overlooked. It is to that group that dissatisfied community members will eventually protest. If board members have not been oriented to the proposed change, they cannot be in a good position to meet protests from the community. Further, in most American communities, boards of education are the official governing groups for public schools, and school officials have the obligation to inform board members of impending or proposed changes in program.

A number of years ago the writer was asked by a science teacher if it would be all right to use the film *Human Growth* in his classes. It was discussed by the staff and the decision was made to proceed cautiously. The film was borrowed for a week and was shown first in staff meeting. Two open meetings of parents saw the film next and then it was taken downtown to the men's University Club. These groups asked numerous questions but there was general support for use of the film in seventh grade science classes. No school class was to see *Human Growth* until the staff was satisfied that its use would be supported in the community.

Among the interested persons present at the University Club program was the superintendent of schools. He gently inquired if any plans had been made to show the film to the board of education. No plans had been made, in spite of the fact that the board was meeting that evening. The superintendent was kind enough (and wise enough) to get a last-minute change in the agenda for the meeting so that *Human Growth* could be included. Needless to say, the staff felt much better the next morning to read in the papers that the board of education supported the school's use of the film.

## Summary

This chapter has stressed these points:

1. Co-operative experience with the school staff should precede parents' involvement in curriculum problems.
2. Parents should share in curriculum discussion before the issues are settled. They should not be expected to give automatic support to plans which they have not helped to consider.
3. Teachers should be resource persons in parent discussion groups.
4. Parent discussion groups should proceed from relatively non-controversial problems into more difficult problems as the success of the groups warrants.
5. Small groups encourage more extensive participation of parents.
6. Parents at times may be invited to work with staff committees.
7. Representative citizens from the community at large may be invited into the school to hear explanations of plans.
8. News and entertainment media are useful as one-way communication in public relations, but additional means must be sought for effective exchange of ideas between school and community.
9. The board of education should share a school staff's plans for curriculum change.

Community support for changes in the school program is a must. How it is to be obtained in a particular school district is a question for the local leadership to decide in light of what is best in that community. If community members are included in school policy making all along, there will be less likelihood of rebellion and uprising when changes are made. Even when no opposition is evident, it is still important for a school staff to know what community people think about the school program, because a faculty ought to be carrying out the type of program which represents the desires and aspirations of the people being served. The superintendent and the board of education members are key persons in community understanding of a school's program. They should be consulted and included in the development of plans for the co-operative consideration of curriculum and curriculum changes by the school staff and the community.

# Chapter 7

## HOW SHOULD THE PRINCIPAL AND STAFF MEET
## SPECIFIC PRESSURE MOVEMENTS FOR
## CURRICULUM CHANGE?

It is becoming increasingly difficult for high school teachers and principals to avoid consideration of curriculum change. If they are not stimulated by their own awareness of inadequacies in their present program to look at the possibility of curriculum improvement, they will be challenged by popular journals, professional conferences, graduate school attendance, and various vocational groups to "do something for the gifted," train more scientists, encourage more of the capable students to prepare for college, increase economic understanding, improve performance in communication skills, persuade more students to take mathematics, establish a core curriculum. These pressures by no means encompass all the demands bearing down on secondary school staffs, but are illustrative of forces both within and outside the profession which tend to question or disturb present-day school programs.

In 1957–1958 the whirling of Sputniks and Explorers about the earth was almost matched by the whirling of charges and counter charges about our high schools. Some people questioned the adequacy of science instruction and the over-all effectiveness of secondary schools. Others were tempted to believe that our schools should make changes to bring them in line with the admired features of Russian schools.[1] The goal of a strong, balanced program was threatened by the exaggeration of actual needs and by the misuse of available information.[2]

Fortunate indeed is the school staff which can show that it is conducting a continuing and comprehensive study of its own offerings and that it is making desirable changes in light of new information and new conditions. Such a school staff does not wait until a local community member telephones the principal to ask what the high school is doing for the gifted or why more students are not taking science. What are the facts locally on questions that disturb many of our citizens? *Is* something being done for the gifted? How many students *are* taking science courses? What *are* counselors doing to encourage capable students to plan for college? Preferably, these questions and others like them should be included in the orderly, continuous evaluation a staff makes of its whole program.

The central advantage of a faculty's continuous study of its curriculum program is the opportunity it provides to achieve balance in outlook and emphasis. If a faculty deals only with pressures as they arise, first one aspect of program and then another may receive disproportionate attention, to the neglect of the program as a whole. Indeed, program modifications which are considered for one subject area or for one group of pupils may have features which affect objectives held for other subject areas or other groups of pupils. It is difficult, for instance, to group one portion of the student body homogeneously without grouping other portions also. The very fact that one portion of the student body (for example, superior students) is set out for separate grouping leaves the remainder of the students more homogeneous in respect to the relative absence or low degree of the quality which the first group is found to possess.

[1] Indeed Russian schools appear to be effective for a Communist type society; that they could hardly be expected to undergird a democratic type society did not occur to some of our people.

[2] See T. M. Stinnett, "Check That Statistic!" *The Educational Record*, April, 1957, 38:2, pp. 84–86. Also see Walter C. Eells, *The School Executive*, March, 1957, 76:7, pp. 42–46.

The writer hopes that he is not misunderstood as opposing programs either for the gifted or for science. The point is that these needs should be considered within the framework of the whole curriculum program and the needs of *all* pupils, if the program is to be effective for all. This is not to say that there will not be times when a faculty is justified in paying special attention to a particular phase of the curriculum program. It is only as particulars are studied and improved that the whole program advances. These particulars should not be approached in isolation from the rest of the program but in relation to it. A staff cannot reasonably assume that the only parts of the school program needing consideration are those items receiving concentrated attention in conventions, journals, and luncheon clubs.

Such pressures as the one for doing more about the gifted students, however, may be employed by a principal to help the faculty look at questions pertaining to a program for *all* pupils. It has already been pointed out that grouping for the gifted opens the possibility of grouping for other pupils. Does the staff consider extensive grouping a desirable arrangement for all pupils? Should grouping pertain to all phases of a program or to just certain subject areas? In seeking answers to such questions as these, a principal not only will want to help his teachers consider research findings but will also want to call their attention to philosophical implications relating to the research and his school's general purposes and objectives.

## Special Classes

If a principal and his faculty decide to set up special classes for the gifted beyond the customary subject areas, they may want to postpone grouping in the subject areas until the results of these classes are studied. If the decision is to try special grouping for the gifted in the conventional subject areas, then a faculty may want to start out in only one or two subject areas until more information can be obtained. Cheltenham High School teachers in suburban Philadelphia have found as a practical matter that gifted pupils rarely are in more than two or three special classes and many are in a special grouping in only one subject.[3] For one thing, pupils are not always equally interested in all subjects, and for another, some pupils do not find it possible or desirable to summon all the time and energy required to meet the cumulative demands of several special classes in which the assignments are lengthy and difficult.

Should pupils who are only high average in native ability but extraordinarily high in good study habits and motivation be permitted to try their luck with a class for the gifted? Should pupils who are very high in native ability but who have poor study habits and low motivation be included in a class for the gifted? Should gifted pupils have the option of remaining with a regular class if they do not want to enter the special group? Should the size of a class for the gifted be the same as that for other classes? Should a class for the gifted try to accomplish all that a regular class does plus additional work, or should it be freed from regular class requirements in order to plan and carry out an entirely new course? Should the length of class time and the number of meetings per week be different for special classes from the schedule for regular classes? These are some of the questions which may arise as a faculty plans and sets up special groups for the gifted.

Acceleration and/or enrichment may pose as many questions, and a faculty, for that matter, may want to try combinations of acceleration, enrichment, and grouping. All the time these possibilities are being considered, a faculty should ponder the potential effects not only upon the gifted pupils but upon the other pupils as well. This pondering should take into account social and psychological relationships in addition to proficiency in mastering subject matter. As plans merge into action, evaluation should be in terms of school-wide effects as well as the achievements of the gifted as a special group.[4]

---

[3] This is also true in Portland, Oregon, high schools.

[4] This brief discussion on educating the gifted may indicate the complexity of the problem and the need for a faculty to make careful study of proposals relating to it.

It is possible, too, that not all the gifted will go on to college and the problem here is not just to guide highly capable pupils into a decision for college but to decide what kind of education the high school should provide for such pupils. Is it sufficient to give them college preparatory work or a general course, or is there a better terminal program which ought to be provided? Can we assume at present that all highly capable pupils should attend college?

## Pressure for College Admission

As the pressure of increasing numbers of applicants for college admission mounts and many pupils (and their parents and teachers) fear the possibility of not getting into the college of their choice or of not getting into *any* college, secondary school leaders may have to exert extra effort to remain calm and steady.[5] The temptation will be strong to overemphasize the desirability of adequate college preparation. Parents will be warned of the difficulty their children may have in gaining admission to college; pupils will be reminded of the desirability of doing their work just so, so that they will earn the marks necessary to put them high on the list of graduates recommended for college. These cautions are understandable and a principal would not be carrying out his responsibility to pupils and parents if he did not apprise them of the facts relating to the college entrance situation. It is to be hoped, however, that the principal will not let his staff members overlook other desirable objectives in a secondary school program as they step up college preparatory activities. Citizenship, age-peer relationships, physical development, music and art appreciation, and the development of value judgments are other aspects of personal growth which are important for the college-bound and all secondary school pupils.

[5] New college students in 1956–57 increased 6.6 per cent over 1955–56. There were 735,065 new college students in the fall of 1956 according to the United States Office of Education.—*Higher Education and National Affairs* (American Council on Education), November 21, 1956, V:25, p. 4.

One interesting means of meeting the needs of gifted students is the Advanced Placement Program of the College Entrance Examination Board in which students take college level courses in high school which are evaluated for advanced credit standing on college entrance.[6] In 1955–56 eighty schools over the country offered courses in this program in twelve subject fields.[7]

## Problems of Program Balance

It has been suggested that the principal should help his staff carry on a continuing evaluation of curriculum structure and content, that he should strive for balance and wholeness in the school program. In spite of seasoned and careful curriculum study, however, a faculty will occasionally be confronted with sincere, interested, and willing community citizens who want to furnish free materials, speakers, courses of study, and evaluation for the favored cause of a club, association, or foundation. It is doubtful that any high school could find enough time in the school year to use all the free instructional materials available to it. It is also doubtful that citizens with favorite causes and free materials would approve the high school's use of *all* available materials. Naturally, they approve the school's use of the material *they* offer. Some of the offers include films, printed tests, assembly speeches, speeches to the faculty, exhibits, demonstrations, and tours of local businesses. It is sometimes difficult for the prospective donor of materials and services to understand a principal's reluctance to accept a generous offer of assistance, especially if local businessmen have agreed in advance to finance the venture.

There will be numerous occasions, of course, when the principal and faculty welcome materials and services which fit into the school's on-going program and are consistent with the school's objectives. Actually, school programs have been enriched by the production of films and other classroom aids by industrial firms

[6] "College Study in High School," *The School Review*, December, 1956, LXIV:9, pp. 386–388.
[7] *Ibid.*, p. 387.

and other business organizations. Films with production costs and techniques far beyond reach of most school systems have been made available to schools in many cases at no more expense than a transportation charge. The writer recently was privileged to sit in a small preview audience which was considering the purchase for many thousands of dollars of a film series which had been very successful on television. A few school persons were guests of a great industrial firm and the public relations officials of this firm wanted only to know that the film series had educational value and practical usefulness before they asked their company to invest money in the series and to furnish the films to the schools without cost. True, the business firm had a selfish purpose, frankly stated, in providing the films for school use. This purpose, which was to encourage more students to become interested in science as a career choice, was not inconsistent with school purposes. Here were the vast resources of a great business concern made available to implement the joint educational objectives of business and school personnel. Such examples of partnership between school personnel and community members are happy circumstances for school-community co-operation.

Nonetheless, the principal is justified in being cautious in regard to high pressure programs with their elaborate brochures (not that good programs cannot have fancy brochures), clever sales pitch, and gentle reminders that all the other good schools thereabouts are signing up for the service (or this campaign is starting with a select few of the better schools in the region). The principal and faculty might do well to establish some ground rules for the use of free curriculum materials and guides *before* a local issue develops. If the problem is critical or frequent in a particular community, it might be wise for the school staff to ask the superintendent and board of education to establish the rules or to approve rules suggested by the faculty. In regard to national contests and activities for high school pupils, the National Association of Secondary-School Principals compiles an approved list.[8]

[8] National Association of Secondary-School Principals, *The Bulletin.* September, 1956, 40:221, pp. 1–8.

## Problems of Motivation

Not all the pressures to change, add to, or take from the curriculum come from without the schools. Like other human activities, school teaching has its trends and its movements. Teachers who have presided at their chalkboards for twenty-five years or more may suspect that teaching has its cycles too. Be that as it may, as a new curriculum movement is started, some school staffs will reject it without critical examination. Later, as the movement becomes a definite trend, some school staffs will adopt it without critical examination.[9] Neither procedure is advisable. Changes in program or structure should make sense in terms of the local situation, especially to the people involved.

Like it or not, teachers do their best work when they are doing what they believe in; it is not sufficient just to have them co-operating. Some teachers become panicky when a marked departure from the conventional curriculum is being considered. Such proposals as the core curriculum may be rejected without a hearing if they are presented without sufficient background information and study. For this reason any decided change in curriculum structure or content should develop from a need which is evident and understood by the school staff and the community.

Even if it is clear that teachers and parents would like to see a curriculum program improved, a comprehensive plan like the core curriculum is not necessarily the answer. Before any such plan is considered, a school staff may want to work first on improving teaching methods within an existing framework of classes. When it is clear that the staff is ready to move into definite changes in the basic structure of classes, it may be advisable to begin by grouping together subject teachers who have the same pupils so that they may share a common planning or conference period. In such a plan it is assumed that the pupils remain in

[9] In a discussion group on the core curriculum at the national meeting of the N. A. S. S. P. in 1956 one principal stated, "Three years ago when I attended one of these discussions on the core curriculum, I was so impressed that I went back to my school and set up a core curriculum right away. Now, I have some questions!"

the same basic block or group throughout the school day, or at least in the major subjects. Scheduling together teachers who have the same pupils but in different subjects may be done on a very small scale, with a minimum of two teachers and one pupil group, or it may be extensive, involving the whole school. Below is an example of this plan with five sophomore groups having the same teachers in four required subjects. During the second period these classes might be in physical education, music, and study hall.

"Little School" of Sophomores

| Periods | Eng. | Math. | Soc. Stud. | Sci. | Elective |
|---------|------|-------|------------|------|----------|
| 1 | 10A | 10B | 10C | 10D | 10E |
| 2 | JOINT CONFERENCE PERIOD FOR TEACHERS OF THESE GROUPS | | | | |
| 3 | 10B | 10C | 10D | 10E | 10A |
| 4 | 10C | 10D | 10E | 10A | 10B |
| 5 | 10D | 10E | 10A | 10B | 10C |
| 6 | 10E | 10A | 10B | 10C | 10D |

If the pupils in the above groups all have the same elective, such as first year Spanish, the elective teacher can be a member of the planning team. The co-operating teachers would meet a minimum of one period per week for planning. These teachers can be given the privilege of reassigning any pupil from any of the A, B, C, D, E classes to any other class in that same grouping. Such "little schools" can do something toward restoring to the large school the advantages of the small school.

An entire school can be organized on such a basis. One variation of the plan is to designate a staff member as an assistant principal of all "little schools" in one grade level or of a third (or any other portion) of the pupils vertically. If a three-year school, for instance, has eighteen sections in each grade level, there could be three "little schools" with six sections each in each grade level. Each "little school" could have its own assemblies, its own lunch period, and in other ways maintain its particular identity.

Obviously, such a plan works more completely on the junior high level, in which most of the classes are required. For those subjects which are required, however, the plan can be used through the twelfth grade. While it would be difficult to schedule minor subject teachers within the joint conference period, they can be included from time to time either by holding the conference meeting after school or by having other teachers cover their classes for the period. This can be very important in certain conference group projects, such as a consideration of pupil behavior characteristics in which the physical education teacher, for instance, sees the pupils in situations somewhat different from those in the major subject classes.

If the school is not large enough to warrant the appointment of a staff member as assistant principal for the "little schools," teacher chairmen in each "little school" can be the leaders. "Little school" faculty groups are excellent proving grounds for teacher orientation and teacher growth. They must, however, have good leadership; otherwise meetings may be scarcely better than complaint sessions about problem pupils. The "little school" plan, like any other technique, will not be better than its leadership. The principal himself should attend the meetings frequently, not only because teachers will profit from his thinking, but because he will profit from knowing his staff better.

Scheduling pupils in larger blocks of time with the same teacher is another possibility which a faculty may want to consider. It should not be undertaken, though, unless it offers an answer to a need or shortcoming felt by the staff. That is, if the staff feels that pupils, in the current arrangement, have too many different teachers, then the large block of time with the same teacher may be the solution. Again, if the faculty feels that two subjects, such as English and social studies, can be taught better when presented together than when taught separately, the large block of time with the same teacher may be the answer.

At the outset, a staff may want only one teacher to try working with the same group of pupils two periods and then have that teacher report on his experiences. Later, if the plan seems satisfactory, others on the staff may be willing to try it. In the junior high school grades a faculty may want a teacher to have the same pupils even longer than two periods. In the seventh grade, particularly, such a plan provides a better transition from the elementary school type of organization to the conventional secondary school type than the chopped-up school day in many seventh grade schedules.

In this plan the subjects taught by the same teacher may be taught either in a unified, interrelated manner or as entirely separate subjects. That is something each faculty will have to work out. Even when the subjects are taught separately to the same group of pupils, the teacher in question will have a much smaller total number of pupils per day to deal with than in the teaching of that many different classes of different pupils. The majority of junior high schools now use some block-time classes in their daily schedule.[10]

Block-time classes make it possible to cross conventional subject lines and even to develop a new organization of subject content. The *core curriculum* by any other name is a little more (but not much more) acceptable to teachers who prefer conventional curriculum organization. Basic learnings, common learnings, and general education are some of the other terms used, although all mean different things in different schools. Some faculties, in order to avoid controversy, simply refer to their block-time classes as English and social studies or by other pertinent subject names.

A description of the core program lists these characteristics:

Providing a large block of time for the study and solution of problems which boys and girls recognize as important.

Using the persistent problems of young people as organizing centers of study.

Employing and organizing the subject matters of many fields in the solving of these problems.

Providing fundamental guidance for young people both in terms of a sense of direction and in the development of a critical, consistent pattern of beliefs and values—each student in his own way.[11]

[10] The National Association of Secondary-School Principals, *The Daily Schedule in 1,250 Junior High Schools*, p. 4. Washington, D. C.: The Association, 1956.

[11] Arno A. Bellack and others, *Preparation of Core Teachers for Secondary Schools*, p. 14. Washington, D. C.: The Association for Supervision and Curriculum Development, 1955.

It should be pointed out that the purposes, forms, and techniques of program plans which are called "core curriculum" vary widely from school system to school system and sometimes from school to school within the same school system. These are some of the respects in which these plans vary:

The extent to which a plan is pre-structured for all core teachers in a building or in a school system.

The extent to which individual core teachers pre-plan their own units of work and the extent to which units of work are developed through working with individual class groups.

The relationship between core classes and other classes.

The relationship between core classes and the guidance program.

The relationship between core classes and student activities.

The relationship between core content and conventional subject content.

The degree of pupil-teacher planning.

The extent to which core is built around youth problems.

The scope or size of the core program in number of periods and in its proportion of the whole school program.

Grade levels in which the core program is offered.

How pupils are grouped for core classes.

Whether core is *available* to all pupils at a given grade level.

Whether core is *required* of all pupils at a given grade level.

The extent to which the core program draws from community resources.

The name given to the core program.

While most core programs draw from a combination of English and social studies, a few schools have set up the core program *in addition* to the existing classes, not replacing any of them. One interesting example is the Thomas Jefferson Junior High School of Fairlawn, New Jersey, where the core curriculum proposes to correlate all subject matter fields by the development of a central theme, which in 1955–56 was "The Building of a Model Community and a Home." In this school the core classes call upon the subject classes for the development of certain skills and knowledge needed to resolve problems being pursued in the core classes.

Any core program which extends throughout a school would have to make provision for considerable variation among teachers in plans and practices. This would permit the more creative teachers to move ahead rapidly and at the same time would not penalize a teacher who feels more secure in keeping some separate identity of English and social studies; there would be certain differences, too, in the degree of pre-planning. Teachers would be in various stages of growth *toward* desired purposes and practices. This organization of a core program that permits a variety of practices would also enable a school to avoid unwholesome competition between core classes and separate English and social studies classes.

However a core program is organized or whatever it is called, its development should be worked out carefully and over a period of time. It will be effective only to the extent that faculty members are thinking and working together. This does not mean that all teachers on a staff must begin core experiences simultaneously, but it does mean that most, and preferably all, teachers on a staff are willing to see the beginners launch forth and to wish them well. Furthermore, these teachers who are participating in the core program, especially when it is in an experimental stage, should communicate their experiences and findings frequently and extensively to the rest of the faculty so that the enterprise will be kept a faculty project instead of a venture of a few bold persons.

## Real Life Problems

Even after a core program has become well established, it is desirable to keep the entire staff up-to-date (and the community too) on the characteristics and signposts of the program. The reason for this is that the core plan, if it is to be effective, will not be static, once change has begun. School marking systems, honor societies, student government organization, activity programs, and other phases of day-to-day school life may be potential areas of change when a core program is in full operation.

In one school the school secretary ushered in five excited ninth grade pupils and the principal greeted them with a smile. "We're a committee from our general education class,"[12] one began.

"Please sit down," the principal said, "and tell me what your committee has in mind." The secretary scooted in an extra chair so that all would have seating space.

"We're studying safety in our community," the spokesman resumed, "and our class thinks the playground situation at our school is dangerous. Before school, at noon hour, and after school our pupils many times run out into the street to get baseballs and we think somebody's going to get hurt."

"What do you think we ought to do?" asked the principal.

"We think a high wire fence ought to be put around the playground," one committee member replied. The principal winced inwardly. He had, he explained to the committee, asked the board of education several times for a playground fence, but so far none had been forthcoming.

"Did you tell them we might have a serious accident in the street someday?" one of the pupils inquired.

"Yes, I did," the principal answered, "and they agreed it ought to be done but said there was no money for it."

"Is there something we can do to convince the board?" the committee asked almost in unison.

"I don't know of anything right now," the principal replied, "but let me think it over and we'll see."

Later that day when the principal talked to the teacher she turned out to be a little more resourceful. "Why don't I have them keep track of the number of times the balls roll into the street and the number of cars that go by every day?" The principal thought this would be a good plan. He didn't have a suggestion of his own anyway.

When the youngsters took their data to the monthly meeting of the board of education, the purchase of the fence was approved within five minutes! Thus did a class not only learn about safety on playgrounds, but it also learned (and taught the school) how

[12] Core classes were called general education classes in this particular school system.

young citizens can influence policy making before they are old enough to vote.

On another occasion a principal had just leaned over his desk to read the morning mail when several members of an eighth grade core class filed in and handed him a note from their teacher. "These pupils have asked a question I can't answer," read the note. "Can you help them?"

On inquiry, two or three of the pupils started talking at once about a locker search that was going on near their room upstairs. "That isn't so unusual," the principal explained. "Somebody probably lost something valuable and thinks maybe it was stolen."

"Is it right to search our lockers without our consent, though?" chorused the pupils.

The principal furrowed his brow. "Well, we haven't asked pupils about that sort of thing before. What started all this?"

"You see," they explained, "we've been studying the Bill of Rights ("Now I know why their teacher sent them to me," thought the principal") and when we came to our homeroom this morning we saw this teacher opening all the lockers. We want to know if that isn't unwarranted search and seizure!"

To himself the principal mused, "Trying to apply the Bill of Rights to themselves, are they? Why aren't they satisfied just to talk about the Bill of Rights?" Aloud he said, with typical administrative skill, "Before we try to answer that question, why don't we get all the facts straight? You go find the teacher and ask just what the locker search was about." (It was learned that a girl had lost her coat.) "Let me know later today." This seemed to make sense, and the pupil committee left the office.

The principal sat down to figure out the next move, for he had a feeling that the pupils would return with their original question. Before he could summon the semblance of an idea, the committee returned even more excited than before. "Now we've done it," they exclaimed.

"Done what?" the principal fearfully asked.

"Made that teacher mad as hops. Said we had no business butting in and she is going to see our teacher about it!"

At this point the principal's long and practical experience came to the fore. "Let me see if I can get the facts," he suggested. "You boys and girls go back to your class and I'll send word to you later what I find out. You may approve of the locker search when you get all the truth about it." There wasn't much conviction in his voice though.

Before the day was over, more than one teacher came into the office "mad as hops." "What's this school coming to," they demanded, "if we have to ask pupils for permission to search the lockers?"

Other teachers were just as excited in the opposite direction. "It's time we put up or shut up," they said. "Either we confine the Bill of Rights to talk-talk or we apply it to our own school life!" Other core classes took up the discussion. Never before had the Bill of Rights generated such interest in that school. Do pupils have rights as citizens? Does history apply to real people or is it just something in books? What privileges should teachers have that pupils should not have? Did the girl who lost her coat have the right to ask for all pupils' lockers to be searched? What rights did a pupil purchase when he paid his locker rental?

In a few days a joint pupil-teacher committee agreed that thereafter when a locker search became necessary, the student council president should be notified and he would accompany the staff member on the rounds of the lockers. Thus, the pupils felt that their rights would be protected. Both the pupils and the faculty accepted the arrangement.

Theoretically, of course, either of the incidents just described could have taken place in a conventional class. That they occurred in core classes was probably due to flexibility in planning, opportunity for intensive pursuit of a problem, and a feeling (encouraged in core classes) that young citizens *can* do something about school and community problems, that there *is* a relationship between what they study and their own individual lives. A faculty, however, has to be flexible and resourceful when such problems come up.

The core program itself has to be flexible and subject to change from its original form and content or it will become just another department with its vested interests and its traditions. To the extent that core program developments are made available to all and all are included in the planning, many difficulties will be avoided or easily solved. Core teachers themselves, however, need more than just the support and encouragement of other staff members. As old patterns of action are discarded, new patterns have to be developed. Resources which to some degree provide help in choice of content and which to a great extent provide help in techniques must be made available to core teachers if the program is to succeed. Although Wright reports that some eighty-eight different institutions of higher learning give pre-service training specifically for core teachers, the fact remains that the overwhelming number of core teachers and prospective core teachers now in the field have not had specific core curriculum training in college.[13] This means that a successful core program must lean heavily upon an intensive and continuous in-service training plan.

As to content and materials of instruction, written guidelines may be of considerable assistance. Teachers themselves may help develop such guidelines. On the techniques of core teaching, however, some in-the-classroom personal help ought to be provided. If the principal is unable to give this kind of help himself, he should have a staff assistant who is qualified and who is given sufficient time to do the work. Actually, core teachers can and do help each other a great deal (as do all good teachers), but in certain matters they will profit from and will appreciate intelligent supervisory assistance. Some of the problems which core teachers should not have to work on alone are:

Techniques of pupil-teacher planning.
Teacher pre-planning.
Criteria for determining when a unit of work should be terminated.
The role of committee work in class.
Working with individual differences of pupils.
The place of class drill in the learning process.
How to develop fundamental skills.

[13] Grace Wright, *Core Curriculum Development, Problems and Practices,* pp. 46–47. Washington, D. C.: U. S. Office of Education, Federal Security Agency, 1952.

How to evaluate progress.
How to relate one year's work to another.
How to increase depth and breadth of pupil interests.
Obtaining satisfactory materials and equipment.

This list of problems illustrates some of the areas in which core teachers should be able to depend upon their leaders for assistance. It goes without saying that a classroom and its equipment should be such as to encourage core teaching. Furniture should be movable; necessary supplies should be on hand or easily obtainable. In many situations it may be desirable for core teachers to be grouped together in the same part of the building so that they can confer and plan together more easily. It may be that the new wash basin in the core teacher's classroom, or the new bulletin board, or the new tables and chairs, or the work alcove are as important as indicators that an administrator believes in and supports the core teacher's work as they are of direct instructional aid. This could be said, of course, of all teaching situations.

At any rate, there is no greater single contributor to the effectiveness of core program development than wholehearted, attentive, and active support and encouragement from school leadership. If a building principal leaves to a supervisor, whether an immediate staff member or one from the city-wide personnel, the whole load of leading and developing the core program, then it is obvious that he has more important things to do and the core teachers will know how important they are. The same can be said of system-wide leaders who never participate in planning sessions at the school unit level. There is no pre-service training however thorough and no in-service training however excellent that cannot be undermined and damaged by unsympathetic or indifferent school leaders.

## Public Understanding

What has been said about participation of parents and other community members in curriculum studies is doubly true for such marked departures from conventional patterns as the core curriculum. It is quite likely that a core program will have features and characteristics which were unknown in the school experience of parents and which therefore are confusing to them, to say the least. When pupils are asked what subjects they are studying and they reply, "Core" or that they don't have subjects, any unkind critic lurking in the shadows may come forth to do battle. For that matter, any friend of the school has a right to know and understand the school's purposes and the school's program. A friendly P.T.A. member once said, "Look, I'm for the school and the teachers and what we're trying to accomplish, and when I'm here in the building I think I understand. My trouble is that when one of my neighbors criticizes the school's program, I don't know how to answer him."

This feeling is perhaps shared by many friends of schools who have not been given sufficient experience in group thinking and planning to become articulate about what they vaguely believe and support. Herein lies one of the greatest challenges to school staffs: to provide the school's friends with the information and understandings which they need to defend the schools against unfair criticism. Unless interested parents are included at certain points in the planning and evaluating experiences of a school staff as a core program is developed, misunderstanding and even opposition are likely to be the result.

## Summary

This chapter has presented some of the pressures for curriculum change, both from within and without the school. The following points were considered:

1. It is difficult for a faculty and principal to avoid consideration of curriculum change.
2. The alert staff does not wait until difficulties arise but carries on a continuing study of its program.
3. A staff should strive for balance in curriculum design; all

phases of the program and the needs of all pupils should be taken into account.

4. Sometimes the study of a particular problem, such as education of the gifted, may enable a faculty to restudy the offerings for all the pupils.

5. In a study of the gifted it may be helpful to start with a few special groups; results can then be evaluated before other plans are made.

6. One of the problems in planning a program for the gifted is how far to go beyond just preparing them for college.

7. Currently increasing enrollments in our colleges may cause some school staffs to neglect other phases of a school program in favor of college preparatory work.

8. Advanced college placement might be considered as one means of meeting the needs of the gifted.

9. One pressure on the secondary school program is the availability of free materials and suggestions from local and national interest groups.

10. Sometimes school staffs accept or reject curriculum proposals without critical examination.

11. Rather than suddenly adopt comprehensive plans like the core curriculum, a staff should first try less ambitious modifications of its program. The "little school" plan can be started gradually and increased as experience warrants.

12. Scheduling pupils in larger blocks of time with the same teacher is a possibility which a faculty may want to consider.

13. The nature of core programs varies considerably from school to school. The entire faculty should accept and understand such a program as it is developed.

14. A core program has to be flexible and subject to change from its original form and content or it will become just another subject department.

15. Core teachers need ample resource and supervisory help.

*16.* The success of a core program depends heavily upon the support and encouragement of school leadership.

*17.* A core program should have the understanding and support of parents.

To what extent should a principal and his staff be influenced by specific pressure movements for curriculum change? Only insofar as such plans fit into the unique needs of the particular school. Local innovations growing out of the teacher's own experiences are far better than the copying of imported plans. Comprehensive changes should be made carefully and with adequate preparation. The wise faculty carries on continuous curriculum study.

# Chapter 8

# HOW CAN THE PRINCIPAL AND STAFF CONTINUE THE BENEFITS WHICH COME FROM CO-OPERATIVE STUDY?

EXPERIMENTATION should stimulate and encourage teachers; it should not make them feel their security is threatened. It has been suggested again and again in these pages that the principal's participation and active leadership in whatever program is developed will go far toward assuring teachers. Above all, the principal should not be the first to exclaim, "That's a very good idea but it just won't work administratively!" If the principal is more inclined to say, "Let's see if we can work it out some way," teachers will respond more readily with "We're willing to give this proposal a try."

If the leader wants staff members to have a receptive attitude toward change, then he himself must have a receptive attitude toward change of administrative matters which are dear to him. In other words, the principal sets the pace by his own example of flexibility, not just in curriculum matters but in school life in general.

Likewise, if the principal wants teachers to take an active part in curriculum planning and be willing to experiment with new plans and new methods, then he must be willing for them to share widely in policy making outside the area of curriculum as well as within it. Are there staff and school system committees on salaries, personnel policies, and teacher welfare as well as on curriculum?

Staff members can encourage one another by being fair-minded toward teachers who are trying something new. Even if a particular teacher does not feel ready to volunteer for a project, he can support and help the teacher who does volunteer. This may mean covering a class occasionally for the volunteer teacher, but more importantly it means showing by word of mouth and other action that the non-volunteer teacher wants the volunteer teacher to succeed. Perhaps the greatest assurance to a teacher participating in a curriculum experiment is the knowledge that the whole faculty wants this particular experiment carried out and wants it to turn out well. His success will not only bring personal satisfaction; it will gratify the other participating teachers as well as those who are not direct participants.

Another means of assurance is for the principal to give full and open credit to individual teachers for their contributions. He will of course avoid referring to "my program" and instead will call it "our program." Successful results of experimentation should receive attention in staff meetings and also in parent meetings. The principal will do well to suggest occasionally that a staff member other than himself be the one to make a public presentation of the school's plans or program. He must, of course, avoid centering all this attention on one teacher or on a small group. All those who have had a share in the work should have a share of favorable attention and praise. If there is writing to be done, the material should bear the names of the teachers who wrote it as well as the superintendent's and the principal's.

Needless to say, another occasion for the principal's assurance is when something goes wrong or does not turn out as planned. The principal should share the responsibility for reverses and should stand ready to help when difficulties arise. He should not insist on a faculty's or an individual teacher's pursuing a course which has produced only negative results. Persistence in a failing and hopeless project or activity can produce serious problems concerning further participation in future activities. It often takes courage to abandon such efforts, but prudence requires that it be done.

## Honest Involvement

The principal ought especially to be sure that teachers who participate in new projects really want to do so. Teachers who by training or temperament are not suited for experiments or innovations should not be forced into such experiences. Sometimes even willingness is not a sufficient criterion. If a teacher goes into a project because he thinks the principal wants him to, he does not necessarily have the background of preparation and outlook which the project needs. Furthermore, he may find after he gets into it that the project is too much for him. If this happens, the principal should be willing to release the teacher from the experiment, thus demonstrating to the faculty that volunteering for experimentation does not doom a teacher to follow through regardless of outcome.

In any case, teachers who do not volunteer for experimental projects or who withdraw from them ought to be accorded the same respect and status on the faculty as those who participate. There should not be any feeling on the part of either the principal or the staff that the most capable persons are participating in a project and that those who are outside the project are the conservatives or the inadequates. A principal's thoughtful consideration of non-participating staff members is an especially important matter with teachers to whom breaking loose from long-established patterns may bring unnecessary frustration. These folk should not be made to feel that they are has-beens.

For that matter, there will be certain phases of some staff experiments in which willing teachers can help without being involved in frightening experiences. For example, a teacher who would be overwhelmed with the prospect of teaching pupils in large blocks of time, might on the other hand be willing to help a pupil committee from a block-time class do research work for the group at large. Another opportunity to call on the non-participating teacher is to invite that teacher into an experimental class as a special resource person at certain junctures of the project. The more staff members involved, even indirectly, in a staff experiment, the more the teachers will consider the experiment to be identified with the whole faculty.

Not only should the principal be careful not to force unwilling teachers into experimental phases of curriculum change; he should be thorough in his study of all possible recruits for the experimental phases, even among teachers who have not indicated a desire to participate. Not all the willing persons raise their hands or speak up in a loud voice. A word of encouragement here and a word of challenge there may produce an additional prospect for the project. Many times a teacher will be pleased to think that the principal and faculty believe he has what it takes to help make the curriculum study a success and will be happy to exert extra effort to achieve this result. The principal may have to draw a fine line between making teachers welcome in a project and being sure no one is pressured against his will and beliefs. This is a risk which must be assumed if participation in curriculum change is to move beyond the "star performers" of a faculty to include an enlarging circle of members. This is one of the reasons why a principal's leadership must be established before he encourages a faculty to embark on a course of extensive curriculum change. Involvement of teachers should be in terms of their understanding, their willingness, and their ability.

Sometimes it is not desirable to wait until there is near unanimity in favor of a course of action. The principal should be sure, however, as decisions are made to try new patterns and new techniques, that any minority group on the staff has had ample opportunity to present and defend its views and that this minority is assured that every effort will be made to protect the thoroughness and fairness of the evaluation. It is desirable that teachers who participate in a staff experiment do so without malicious criticism from fellow staff members. If those who have misgivings about the proposed project are assured that *their* status is not threatened, they are likely not to threaten the status of the participating teachers.

Another means of giving assurance to a staff is provision of adequate resources for carrying out the experiment. Teachers who are willing to try new methods and new organizations should receive sufficient help in the way of materials, equipment, and training to make their experiences satisfying and fruitful. Their class-rooms should be arranged to furnish the flexibility which the experiment requires; the necessary texts and reading materials should be on hand; and there should be ample time in their work week for careful planning. It has already been suggested that supervisory assistance, both in the school itself and from system-wide personnel, can do much to make a staff project successful and rewarding. Above all, a participating teacher should not be left to feel that he is abandoned to his own resources as soon as he assumes his task. He should feel that others are in the project with him and that he will receive the help which he needs.

As staff members are willing to leave the security of the known for the uncertainty of the experimental, they need another kind of assurance to take its place. This assurance can come from their knowing that participation is voluntary, that the status of those who do not participate is not threatened, that credit is given where credit is due, and that material and supervisory resources are avail-able. Most of all, participating teachers will feel assured if they know that what they are working at is what the staff *wants* and is willing to see through to satisfactory completion.

## Broadening the Base of Involvement

After a staff has seen the early phases of an experimental program carried through to satisfactory development, it may want to see the plan extended to include other teachers and other classes. The principal and staff must carefully decide when an experimental program should become a new pattern. In the initial phases of a curriculum experiment, when the full impact of its implications has not been realized, issues may not be sharply drawn. There is a certain satisfaction, too, in doing something new and in receiv-ing favorable attention for early successes. After the excitement of getting the project underway is replaced by the need for main-taining continuing achievements and satisfactions, what happens, for example, when an experimental class settles down to its day-to-day experiences? When the new wears off, will the experimental group continue to bring gratifying results, or will unexpected problems raise doubts about the experiment's ultimate success?

If the new class moves along without particular difficulty and achieves certain stability, there must be further evidence that its advantages are greater than those of the previous conventional pattern. One of the premiums an experimental group has to pay is that it not only must do well the new things it sets out to do but must do equally well the tasks which were paramount with the type of class which it supplanted. If a block-time class, for example, develops an intensive unit of study pertaining to a community problem, one in which pupil interest is high and continuous and in which outcomes are noteworthy, this class must still do as well on a standardized history test as a conventional class which has been able to concentrate fully on traditional subject matter.

On the other hand, a block-time class may effect certain economies in learning because the learning experiences may be related more directly to pupils' interests and because there may be a greater control of the time allotted to specific tasks. If the need becomes apparent for a class to concentrate much of its attention and effort on a particular shortcoming, the control of time allotment within the block of time will enable teacher and class to do so. This should be done, of course, without neglecting other desired objectives. If the new type class draws from two subject areas, especially if one of them is English, there should be many opportunities for planning learning experiences which are related to both fields.

Another economy should be effected from the block-time teacher's improved acquaintance with the strong and weak points of his individual pupils. Because his total load of pupils per day is less and because his pupils are with him a greater portion of the school day, the block-time class teacher is in a much better position to know his individual pupils and their needs than is the teacher of conventional one-period classes.

In the new type classes, then, much of the information and skill emphasized in conventional classes will be acquired by pupils as they pursue units of study which they and their teacher have planned. It is assumed, too, that the interests and needs of society will not be ignored; real teaching skill is involved in relating an individual's needs to society's needs. If careful teacher-teacher planning has been teamed up with skillful pupil-teacher planning, the level of achievement in the commonly designated fundamental skills and knowledge should be satisfactory. If deficiencies in pupil achievement exist, they ought to be attacked by teacher and class as a necessary and desired job to be done. In other words, here is a life problem on which pupils need help. Pupils in newer curriculum organizations can have their accomplishments evaluated just as well as those in the conventional.

Another phase of the planning problem is the temptation, in a class which has been freed from course of study requirements, for teacher and pupils to engage in a long-drawn-out pursuit of a few intensely interesting and rewarding units of study to the neglect of other desirable and needed studies. How and when to terminate units of work is every bit as important as how to select the units in the first place. As old patterns are discarded, new ones will have to be evolved. There is so much to learn and so much to do that no group of learners can do it all. Choice there must be, but obligation there is too. The choices should be made in terms of criteria and goals (and these obviously must be known and recognized by the persons doing the choosing) and the obligation is to assist each individual to grow toward competent, mature, and responsible citizenship.

In other words, securing freedom from the restrictions of the older type of curriculum is only part of the story. The other part is that the freedom is not just *from;* it is also *for*—freedom for more creative teaching and learning. Structure for the newer types of curriculum program does not necessarily have to be built in terms of rigidly defined portions of knowledge nor do mutually exclusive claims on certain segments of learning have to be staked out by grade level teachers or subject area specialists. This does not free a staff, however, from the responsibility of establishing a structure of desired understandings, concepts, attitudes, competencies, and appreciations which the staff plans to help pupils achieve. Previous experiences of pupils, their apparent capacity for and rate of growth, and their relative progress toward their goals and the school's goals are factors to be included in a staff's planning of work for a specific period of time. As additional teachers agree to participate in newer curriculum organizations originally tried by a few, they will need to be inducted into the new structure, new methods, and new outlook which develop from the try-out experiences.

When the new class achieves the conventional as well as its new goals in an acceptable manner, it still has other hurdles to clear. The manner in which the pupils for the new class were chosen, the special equipment the classroom may have, the special training the teacher may have received, the special supervisory assistance provided by the administration, and the special attention given the class may be matters which other teachers feel would also enhance conventional classes if they could thus be treated. All of this accentuates the desirability of seeing that an experimental class is carefully set up, is accepted by the whole faculty, is evaluated thoroughly, and is operated with somewhat normal equipment, supplies, and services. It has been suggested earlier in this monograph that a teacher of an experimental group should not be asked to carry on without resources and assistance. It is just as true that the experimental teacher should not have exceptional advantages of work load, equipment, and services.

As the first tryout groups prove their merit, others may be set up in the following semester or in the following school year. To the extent that the experimental groups are different in pattern of organization and practice from the conventional classes, the complex problems the staff will have to face in setting up additional groups will increase. If the project involves all of a subject area or a combination of subject areas, then additional teachers from such subject areas will have to be recruited as new groups are formed. The enthusiasm and willingness of these new recruits should be comparable to those qualities in the teachers of the initial groups. They will be if, from the outset, staff members in general have been kept in touch with the purposes, the activities, and the achievements of the experimental classes.

As additional classes are set up along the lines of the original tryout groups, the faculty will have to decide to what extent each class will be encouraged to pursue its own course and to what extent the new type classes will be expected to deal with problems common to all the classes and agreed upon by all. Just as in the conventional classes, it will be discovered that what succeeds admirably in one class with one teacher may be quite difficult to achieve in another class with another teacher. There will be need for agreement on the materials and body of information required of all the classes. Teachers can share responsibility for developing units of work for their classes and for exchanging their findings and materials.

All of this means that before a faculty decides that an experimental program should become a new pattern, it must be sure that the experimental phase has met the objectives set for that phase and that the faculty has the willingness and the resourcefulness to extend the program.

As new methods and materials are developed, as certain groupings and sequences of units of work become successful, as more and more teachers are willing to work in the experimental groups, as fewer and fewer parents and pupils request the conventional classes, a point will be reached when the new type classes are in the majority and the staff may decide to abandon completely the older form of organization in favor of the plan which has proved itself in practice.

When this point is reached, either all the teachers in the subject areas encompassed in the new type classes will become participants in the program or the assignment of those who should not be participants will have to be changed to some other subject field. Mention has already been made of the need for the principal to see that those who take part in a new program have the willingness and ability which the program requires. It is recognized here, of course, that it is possible for a new type curriculum plan to include a wide range of teacher performance. A conventional teacher may find it possible to participate in the new organization of classes, for instance, without giving up his accustomed ways of working. He may, if left to his own devices, draw a hard and fast line between two subjects which he teaches the same group of pupils.

Nonetheless, if the new class organization involves large blocks of time, extensive teacher-teacher planning, and new instructional materials, the conventional teacher who shares in the program will be under pressure and influence which will continue to threaten his customary ways of planning and working. If he can adjust to the influence of the project and modify his procedures, well and good. If he finds this adjustment difficult, other teachers in the new organization may have to make reasonable allowances for deviation from group policies and procedures.

The important factor is the good will and co-operation of all teachers associated in a new curriculum plan. After all, teachers in conventional plans have not necessarily thought or taught alike. There is no point to be gained in merely trading one orthodoxy for another. There should be allowance in the new plan for reasonable differences in teaching practices. Here again, the principal is involved in a delicate balance of leadership. He must, on the one hand, challenge his staff to move forward; on the other, he must protect both the adventurous teacher who runs ahead and the timid one who lags behind. He may caution one and encourage the other, but he will not insist on their being what they cannot be. Above all, curriculum reorganization should not pit one group of teachers against another. Careful planning should prevent such a development, especially if teachers are not moved from conventional ways of working to newer patterns more rapidly than their skills and outlook warrant. This type of problem should be thought about early in a new development and should not be allowed to emerge from careless planning.

### Orientation of New Teachers

As for teachers who are new to the staff, their ability and willingness to participate in the newer class pattern should be ascertained as a condition of employment. That is, the prospective teacher in the subject fields covered by the new classes should have the new plan explained to him so that he will understand the type of work expected of him. This is not to say that the new teacher cannot be trained for the new program but rather that he should indicate his willingness to take part. Granted that some new teachers may change their minds about the desirability of the program after they have experience in it, it will be even worse if the disappointed and disappointing teachers have not had the school's program explained to them before employment.

As new patterns emerge, the principal and staff should remember the need to orient and reorient new groups of teachers and parents to these patterns, year by year, lest serious misunderstanding develop between those who originally worked out the program and those who come in later contact with it. This is perhaps the responsibility most often forgotten in school systems and one which, if neglected, can cause a great deal of trouble.

Some three years after the experience with *Human Growth,* related on pages 63–64, the writer had a request from a mother that her daughter not be required to study that particular unit or to see the film. This mother indicated that her minister had advised all his parishioners to forbid their children to see *Human Growth.* The writer immediately got in touch with the minister, who freely acknowledged that he was waging battle against the film's use, even though he had not seen the film himself.

In the next few days the writer spent virtually all his time answering protesting telephone calls from that minister's congregation. The original orientation of the staff and community in regard to the film's use had been quite complete and quite satisfactory, yet three years later, serious difficulty arose because people who were new to the school community did not have the benefit of that orientation.

It is easy to overlook the intensive in-service training received by original participants in a new program as compared with the amount of in-service activity carried out for later participants. Often original members of a new program are sent to college conferences or classes, or university consultants are employed to help initiate the new plan. In either case, it is unlikely that the school system is able to spend as much money orienting new teachers in the group as it did on the initiation of the new program. If written guides are made available, the new teacher in an experimental program will not be entirely at sea, though these guides will probably need careful explanation and interpretation. Ideally, the secondary school which puts a new type of program into operation should have a helping teacher or curriculum assistant on the staff who is available to work intensively with new teachers in the program. Such a staff member, of course, would be available also to assist other teachers, but his first responsibility would be to the new members.[1]

Another reason for reorientation and re-examination is that the new program will not mean the same the second year or later as it did in the beginning. Certain objectives which seemed paramount at the outset may turn out to be impossible to achieve or undersirable. A new seventh grade program, with which the writer was associated, included in its first year of complete operation provision for rather flexible grouping of pupils.[2] In the planning stage this provision was discussed at length and apparently was going to be one of the interesting features of the program. As the program got under way, however, it soon became evident that the need of seventh grade pupils for stability within a group was much greater than the need for frequent change of group membership. The writer recalls that in several of the conference meetings of the seventh grade teachers, everyone had a more or less guilty feeling because no one was making any progress toward flexibility of group membership in spite of the fact that provision for it was made in the school schedule. The teacher group finally decided to drop this particular objective altogether, simply because it proved in this case to be an unwise procedure.

[1] See also page 41.
[2] A year's faculty-wide study, plus another year's planning by a special committee, preceded the initiation of this program. Teachers in the new program elected their own chairman, a new one each semester. There was also a curriculum assistant on the staff who, together with the principal, worked with the teachers in their daily planning period. A system-wide supervisor assisted with the planning.

In another situation a tenth grade program was built around co-operative planning of English, social studies, and science teachers. Conference periods were set up in the schedule so that these teachers could all meet together one period each day. This plan was followed for two years and then was modified because it was not as productive for science teachers as expected. This is no indication whatever that other schools would have this same experience; such co-operative planning groups have been successful in many schools. It is an illustration, however, that each school or each school group will have unique successes and failures which will require occasional re-examination of goals and readjustment of procedures.

In addition, certain individual teachers will report greater or less degree of success in carrying out agreed upon goals than other teachers in the group. Extensive pupil committee work, with the aim of increasing pupil responsibility, may be highly successful with one teacher but somewhat questionable with another. Again, some teachers will lean much more heavily upon pre-planning and upon written guides than will others. This may mean that in some situations a principal or a helping teacher will need to advise a staff member not to pursue a certain course, even though originally it was one of the group's goals. This illustrates the need not only for continuous evaluation and restatement of group goals, but also for abundant supervisory assistance.

One of the interesting developments to observe as a new curriculum program settles down and becomes well established is the tendency for certain materials and ways of working to become standardized. This is quite natural and understandable; in fact, it is necessary if a program is to have unity and stability. Teachers who find certain practices productive will pass the information on to others.[3] If others likewise find these practices desirable, such practices will tend to become standard in all similar groups. Super-

[3] One teacher, skilled in pupil-teacher planning, was puzzled over the remarkable interest, in three successive years, of her classes in a certain optional unit in science. Investigation showed, among other things, that other pupils, especially brothers and sisters, were advising these pupils to be sure to insist on this particular unit when they got in this teacher's class.

visory workers will also report on successful procedures which they observe and other teachers will take up the approved procedures. Furthermore, conference meetings of the teachers involved in the new program will produce recommendations and agreements which all are committed to follow. Teachers of tenth grade block-time classes may have agreed that each class will co-operate in producing a school assembly observing Columbus Day. It may be discovered that this is such a unifying and motivating experience for the tenth grade that it is repeated the second year and then the third. The same group of teachers may have decided also that it is helpful to get a 75-word spelling list well conquered by the sophomores before Thanksgiving vacation.

Someday someone is going to ask Why? in regard to some custom or standard practice of the new program, and if someone else isn't careful, the answer may be, "Why, we've always done it this way." Then the new program is definitely established; it has a tradition. It also has an echo, but the echo may be a little embarrassing; someone may remember hearing it when consideration was first given to breaking away from the previous curriculum pattern.

So long as the customs and traditions serve useful and desirable purposes, no one should complain. If, however, the reason for the customs has been obscured, then a re-examination is in order. As Miel says:

> It is not always easy to determine when a constellation of habits in an educational institution is making for a desirable economy of effort and providing a useful basis of continuity to individual and group living, or when it represents an area concerning which all thinking has stopped and which is serving as a deterrent to constructive action.[4]

A new pattern of action may become just as loaded with custom and inertia as the program which it supplanted. In addition, it will have the added weight of more recent sanction. On the

[4] Alice Miel, *Changing the Curriculum,* p. 1. New York: D. Appleton-Century Company, 1946.

other hand, there is no necessity for abandoning method or content which continues to prove effective just because of long standing. The whole point is that a new type of program may be as subject to powerful convention and tradition as was an older program. This is why the principal and staff should set up safeguards against a newer program's becoming crystallized. Careful and frequent evaluation should enable the staff to identify unsatisfactory content or procedures and to eliminate them. It should also enable the staff to extend and deepen the productive and significant features. Thus, a built-in protection against obsolescence can be set up so that continued change will be gradual and will occur as needed. This is much better than letting a program, once established, rock along until some inadequacy or failure becomes so painful or costly that a thorough revision or rebuilding is required.

Indeed, it should be made clear that the establishment of a new program in the first place should, with few exceptions, provide for smooth and gradual transition from the old method and content to the new method and content. The emphasis should be on program *improvement*. Improvement is never complete nor final; it should be a continuous process. Slow and steady progress, clearly understood and accepted, is much better than striking developments which have to be defended against rejection or misunderstanding and drastically modified or curtailed when achievements fall short of expectations. Co-operative faculty study, once begun, should not be shelved but should be turned toward solution of other school problems which in turn will appear to demand top attention. True, there will be occasions on which marked progress is indicated and achieved in certain respects, but even this marked progress should have back of it slow and careful preparation. Courage to change should be accompanied by keen insights and discerning judgments. Above all, the pace of change should be in step with the faculty's growth in democratic working relationships and skills in applying group thought and action to the achievement of understood and desired goals.

## In Conclusion

To safeguard the continued benefits, then, which come from co-operative study, these factors should be taken into account:

1. Experimentation should stimulate and encourage teachers rather than be a threat to their security.
2. Full credit should be given to individual teachers for their contributions to new programs.
3. The principal should be sure that teachers who participate in new projects really want to do so.
4. As decisions for new plans are adopted, care should be taken to protect the rights of the minority.
5. Adequate resources should be provided for teachers in new experiments.
6. The principal and staff must carefully decide when an experimental program should become a new pattern.
7. Thought must be given to ways of helping the participating teacher who clings to the techniques and outlook of the former program.
8. New teachers should have the new program explained to them before employment.
9. As new patterns emerge, orientation and reorientation of parents and teachers must be provided year by year.
10. New programs may become as subject to convention and tradition as were older programs.
11. Emphasis should be on program improvement; it is never complete nor final; it should be a continuous process.

This monograph has set forth the belief that the greatest challenge to a principal's leadership is the improvement of instruction. The principal and his staff should work co-operatively and democratically toward goals which are understood and accepted by the staff at large. These goals should be sought through study problems which are real concerns of teachers. Change in curriculum pattern should be contemplated within the framework of school system policy and procedure, community understanding and support, and a staff's sense of the school's role in its community. Dynamic and shared leadership can make curriculum study an exciting adventure in group achievement, an adventure leading to a better school program. Such is the challenge to the secondary school principal's courage, skill, and vision.